Wilts & Somerset
A Railway Landscape

The old Great Western Railway shakes
The old Great Western Railway spins –
The old Great Western Railway makes
Me very sorry for my sins.
                    Distant View of a Provincial Town – *John Betjeman*

St. Mary's Church and the town of Bruton seen from the Wilts, Somerset & Weymouth line on St. George's Day 1906. On July 2nd the line became part of the Great Western's Direct Way to the West.
Previous page – narrowing the gauge at Melksham in 1874.

Melksham & District Historical Association.

WILTS & SOMERSET
A Railway Landscape

Duncan Harper

Millstream Books

Raylilway Papers
Mr Sturge Dalmeston
1847

Published 1987
Millstream Books
7 Orange Grove
Bath BA1 1LP

ISBN 0948975040

Text set in 12/12½pt Garamond
Typeset by The Matthews Wright Press Ltd.,
52 Furnham Road, Chard, Somerset TA20 1AP

Printed in Great Britain by Netherwood Dalton & Co.,
Bradley Mills, Huddersfield HD1 6PG

Preface

The tract of Somerset countryside from the Avon valley around the Wiltshire border in the north, to the Cary lands approaching the Dorset border in the south, is one of enchanting contrasts. Wooded combes and downs turn into gentle grassy pastures. Old colliery communities and factory towns become dairy farms and spreading meadows. Across them and through them in the mid-nineteenth century came the railway, marching inexorably from town to town – cross-country lines wandering dreamily to the sea, branch lines carrying away valuable minerals, fast through lines reaching to London. From the deep dark coal-pits of Countess Waldegrave to the open green fields of Farmer Brown, this book celebrates and documents the railways that once abounded in this luscious countryside – the way they were built, the effect they had on the landscape and its inhabitants, and finally the way they died.

Trains still run along practically all of the old Wilts, Somerset & Weymouth line. But other railways like the Somerset & Dorset are now just green lanes, demolished bridges and the occasional virginia-creepered viaduct bestriding a valley…

Contents

RAILWAY LANDSCAPE
An Introduction

The origin of the railway can be found in the meanest footpath. Man beat his tracks in order that he might travel, carry burdens, explore, connect his places, his towns and his factories. He threw stones into muddy gullies and trod them in, generation after generation, and always someone before him had walked, toiled with his produce, driven his beasts or made his pilgrimage. He made ways along hilltop ridges, down into the valleys, beside rivers and across them. He required the earth to yield to his needs and he quarried it to strengthen his ways. He fashioned stone and timber after the nature of the materials, he made monuments of his bridges and he built his canals and railways with ever more vigour, modelling the land to guide them.

The railway came to Somerset in 1840. It was a phenomenon of the age, the child of a revolution and, in time, its principal driving force. This challenging display of initiative in coal production, iron and steel making, cotton spinning and the application of steam power, began in various parts of Britain where coal lay beneath the hills. South Wales, the West Midlands, County Durham, and the North West were the hot beds of the revolution and North Somerset too had her own difficult little coalfield lying deep underground. The enigmatic structures of pre-history in West Wiltshire, the magical Arthurian prospects of Cadbury, the battle-weary marshes of Sedgemoor, the mystical mists of the Isle of Avalon and the classical Roman treasures of Aquae Sulis all played host to a new exploitation of the land. And with the impetus set up by this industry, new ways and means of communication developed: the canal, the steam locomotive, the railway.

The railway succeeded a progression of paths and ways made for men, animals, waggons and boats. But the development of the simple road shows, amid such transitoriness, how lasting and yet how fragile are the monuments that man builds to his own ingenuity. Traces of ancient British trackways and splendid Roman engineering remain to remind us. Out of the neglect of the Middle Ages the roadmaker has struggled with rutted, waterlogged tracks and with varying standards of construction and maintenance, to create the high-speed motorways of today. Yet these may fall again into the familiar disrepair and ruin associated with antiquity, a fate we have provided for much of the railway system in recent years.

Opposite – The meanest footpath ... originally a rope-worked tramway, built c1808, from the stone quarries at Bathampton Down descending to the Kennet & Avon Canal in the valley 500 feet below. The stone sleeper blocks, onto which the rail chairs were bolted, can still be clearly seen.

Paradoxically the railway sowed the seeds of its own decline. It served the men who developed its successors, and as a result of its own short term achievements, too large and haphazard a system was built for its own long term survival. The railway map today is about as extensive as it was in the 1850s, and covers by and large the same ground as then. And though the needs of the population and the functions of the railway have changed radically in the meantime, the continuity of its mark upon the face of the land is assured.

This fine view taken near Limpley Stoke in the 1870s shows the single broad gauge line of the Great Western Railway curving gracefully up the valley. A southbound train can just be made out in the station to the left. The Kennet & Avon Canal clings to the opposite slope.   Wiltshire Libraries

In the same way as a river will take the easiest or quickest route from its spring in the hills to the sea, so low technology routeways follow natural courses determined by the topography of the land traversed. The expense of large scale civil engineering required by more sophisticated route forms has to be commercially or socially justifiable before a canal, a railway or a motorway is allowed to march heedlessly across valleys and through mountains. Many valleys contain their original natural routeway, the river and, alongside, its successors: the track, the metalled road, the canal and the railway. Frequently where one of these becomes abandoned through want of use, it is taken over by the next in line. A railway is superimposed on an old canal bed, or a by-pass laid in a derelict railway cutting. Many Somerset railway routes are now green tracks, interrupted only by broken bridges, filled-in tunnels and burgeoning brambles. Some lines still bear their unremunerative but unremitting traffic, but most are lost, claimed back by the earth, become again part of that mysterious landscape of the past.

Ultimately the green and hilly inland parts of eastern Somersetshire were well served by the Two Railways. They met in the lush undulating country of the southern borderlands. They crossed one over the other on high arches of brick, or low spans of steel, in the woody valleys of the northern districts. They paced each other side by side and they wooed their passengers at rival stations in the same towns. At the turn of the century it was said that there was hardly a corner of Somerset beyond half-a-dozen miles of a railway station.

In a distance of twenty-five miles between the city of Bath and the Iron Age hill fort of Cadbury Castle, the Somerset & Dorset Railway and the Great Western Railway became fatefully intertwined and they met no fewer than seven times. Their relationship in the board room was starchy. Old wounds cultivated suspicions, and perhaps it would not be too fanciful to describe their story as a tragedy, touched with dramatic irony.

They began as blood relatives: the Great Western had many, both overt and closet. Some were as brothers, others as children. The Somerset Central Railway which grew up to become the Somerset & Dorset, was a sort of nephew. Nepotism would have secured the youngster a pedestrian role in the family firm. Ambition however, and bankruptcy, deceitful liaisons and, if it were possible, a measure of pride led to the downfall of the rake, a hero nonetheless, being after all only a captive of circumstance. The upstart was well loved by many, and it is surely not idle to speak in this way of such an apparently inert object as a railway, for it was really the men and women who worked this very special line who gave it life. The Somerset & Dorset and the Great Western, for all that their characters lay in their appearance in the landscape and their distinctive manners of operation, were what they were because of the people who made them so. It was essentially a human drama, and what a record of man's cunning it has left upon the Somerset countryside!

In Bath, the Two Railways were settled in grand stations of local stone on opposite sides of the city. The Jacobean ogee curves of Brunel's façade for many years masked a timber gabled roof over the Great Western platforms. The neo-Palladian mansion built by the Midland Railway and used partly by the Somerset & Dorset, gave proudly onto a concourse arched over with steel and glass. By a neatly hidden bridge on the western outskirts of the city, the S&D crossed over the Great Western in a momentary encounter, turning sharply out of the city and up into the hills to the south.

Beyond lies Midford, a village of virtually no size at all nestling in the next valley, so small that its inhabitants might find themselves in one of five different parishes, having none of its own. Here the brook, which changes its name according to the nearest village, and the Somersetshire

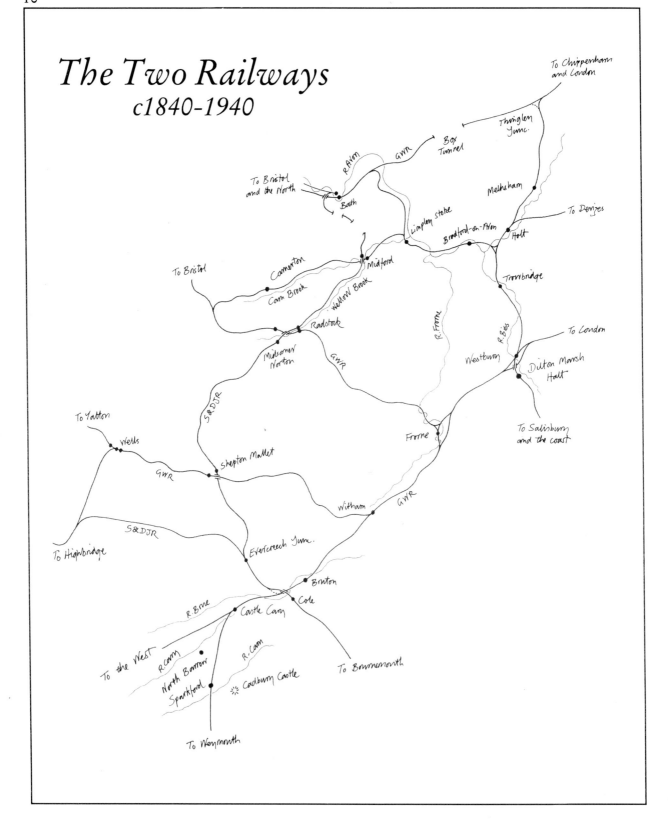

The Two Railways
c1840-1940

Coal Canal were both crossed by the turnpike road. These in turn were crossed by the Great Western's branch to Camerton, and finally they were all surpassed by the S&D which strode upon eight lengthy arches across the valley. The fragile wooden S&D station clung to the western slope for ninety-two years, whereas the Great Western's tiny halt, used for only four brief years before the First World War, lay safely down by the brook.

A few miles further on, at Radstock, the Two Railways approached along neighbouring valleys and converged to within thirty feet of each other. They ran parallel for a way, the S&D steepening gradually until with a haughty gesture it swept high over the Great Western's North Somerset line on a massive five arch structure, and climbed further into the Mendips. The two stations, side by side, filled Radstock with their important presence. At nearby Midsomer Norton the two stations contented themselves with being a brisk walk in opposite directions from the town centre.

A double-headed Bournemouth express climbs out of Radstock S&D station. On the right is the GWR line to Bristol. The locomotives are 2P 4-4-0 No 40568 and Standard class 5 4-6-0 No 73049, photographed on April 12th 1958, by R.E. Toop.

Some miles to the south, over the brow of the Mendips and ranged along its southern flank, are several ancient communities, Axbridge, Cheddar, Wells, Shepton Mallet. The Great Western took ownership of a pair of lines which ran between them, reaching towards Bristol at one end and a fast route to London at the other. The Somerset & Dorset also approached this area with two lines, one its main line from Bath which served Shepton, the other a short branch from Glastonbury to Wells. At Shepton the Great Western crossed over its rival on an obliquely angled bridge of brick and steel spans, while at Wells there was a most unusual conjunction. As to stations, the Great Western inherited two at Wells which for a short period hemmed in the S&D's branch terminus between them. Subsequently, Great Western trains passed right through the S&D goods yard on the level, then into the S&D station and out the other side with some arrogance and, more than likely, a deal of self-satisfaction.

The final meeting occurred some way beyond the Great Western station at Bruton on the Wilts, Somerset & Weymouth line, and shortly before the S&D one at Cole. Here, while the Somerset Central, having crossed the Somerset levels, was as yet undecided whether to be a broad or narrow gauge line and thus, whether to remain on good terms with the implacably broad Great Western or to seek fortune elsewhere, here on the banks of the Brue a junction between the Two Railways had been planned. This sociable scheme however was shrugged off when the Somerset Central, wilful, ambitious and independent, forged ahead, crossed over the Wilts, Somerset & Weymouth, met up with the Dorset Central and changed its title.

In this way the Somerset & Dorset came of name and age, and thereafter the Two Railways plotted their separate Machiavellian paths. The S&D climbed the Mendips as we have seen and, finding itself financially embarrassed but unwilling to seek reconciliation with its former master, leased the line to the South Western and the Midland and entered local folklore. The Great Western had assumed a fatherly prerogative to cover the West Country in broad gauge railways and prospered, largely on account of its trunk routes. The delightful cross-country and branch lines, usually built by local or satellite companies, always found themselves caught up in the larger political railway game. The S&D consisted entirely of cross-country and branch lines; country people have had to fight for their railways. They fought to have them built, and they fought again to save them as the last trains ran.

And so, in the final twist of the story, the Two Railways were almost eliminated from eastern Somersetshire by the brutal march of time and progress. We will come to the Somerset & Dorset, but we begin almost at the beginning with the Wilts, Somerset & Weymouth Railway which remains to this day. By the 1960s the Railway Age had had its sport, and the appearance of the landscape had been irrevocably altered in many ways by its earthworks, it structures and its tracks. And though the story is not yet finished, we will draw to a close at this period when the Two Railways were about to relinquish for ever their grip on our way of life.

PART 1

On this earth 'tis sure
We men have not made
Anything that doth fade
So soon, so long endure:
Roads – *Edward Thomas*

1

KING ARTHUR'S COUNTRY

The gently-rolling grassy landscape of south-east Somersetshire is a sure sign that this is dairy farming country. For countless years, beside the headwaters of the Cary, along the banks of the Brue and the Cam, between the shadows of Cadbury Castle and Glastonbury Tor, the unhurried cattle have grazed. The Cam, meaning "crooked", gave its name to the village of Queen Camel and perhaps even to Camelot itself, if only we knew for certain where those legendary ramparts lie buried. As to the advent of the railway into this peaceful land of Shorthorn and Friesian, it was fairly soon marked on the map. Here however, unlike less charmed or more resourceful areas, it did not inflict its wounds of depopulation or of disfiguring industrial growth too harshly. Milk, butter and cheese are still significant products of this largely rural district.

There was an inevitability in the arrival of the railway here, for this was a natural crossing point for latent, long dreamt-of routeways. The Roman Fosse Way from Lincoln to Ilchester and the south coast ran this way. Having passed through Bath and over the Mendip hills, it crossed the Cary lands, bridging the River Cary near Babcary. At the prominence of Beacon Hill just north of Shepton Mallet, this road was intersected by another, along which lead was transported from the Mendip mines towards Salisbury and Winchester. Coming down from the Ridgeway in the north east was a green road, which from Jack Straw's Castle on the watershed of the Brue and the Stour, as far as Cadbury Castle, is known as the Hard Way. This too continued into Dorset. Who knows the true age of these highways?

Inevitably, Victorian commercial interests, with the new-found power of finance capital, were keen to exploit the potential of such routeways, to link the channels from north to south and to link the capital in the east with the West. The rush to build railways in the mid-1830s and then again in the mid-1840s led to much squabbling, particularly where the routes were obvious and the interests of the promoters conflicting, which they usually were.

'This line,' says the *Tourist's Guide to Somersetshire*, describing in 1894 the Wilts, Somerset & Weymouth, the first railway to penetrate the heart of the area, 'this line traverses one of the prettiest districts in the county, wholly pastoral, plentifully lined and dotted with trees, and diversified with frequent hills.'

A view across the Cary Lands looking west. The village lying in the centre middle distance is North Barrow.

When the railways first came, country areas like this were entirely at the mercy of business interests in the large cities and towns. If a railway were to be built, what countryman would dare to say from which direction it would come or to which town it would lead? Scheme after scheme with London offices in Poultry or Parliament Street offered lines in those early years, marked here and there in coloured inks across the map of the countryside. By and large however, the most obvious commercial links and the most geographically logical routeways that were promoted in the 1820s and 30s were the ones that outlasted the many bubbles, speculations and financial depressions, and were eventually built. These were also likely to be the ones still in use a hundred and fifty years later.

'The south-east borderland of Somerset is a countryside of low, grassy hills which have an extraordinary charm of colouring and atmosphere' wrote Maxwell Fraser in the Great Western's volume *Somerset* of 1934, 'particularly in the neighbourhood of Castle Cary, where every hill-top commands a glorious view of lush green pasture-lands...Little wonder this countryside has a quiet beauty breathing a serenity all too rare in this age of hurry and bustle, for it is the very heart of King Arthur's Country.'

Arguably the greatest change in this landscape in the last two thousand years has been that wrought by the railway. And the romantic notion of Arthur persists ever more strongly and with increasing archaeological justification, despite the scorn of the cynic. According to the *Tourist's Guide*, Cadbury Castle, a vast earthen mound looming to the east of the railway at Sparkford, is merely 'one of the many spots absurdly identified with the myth of King Arthur as the fabled Camelot'. Nearby Castle Cary is described as a 'pleasant little town…' though 'it has never been of importance since the days of Stephen', and that was in 1138 when there really was a castle there, to which the King laid siege.

Castle Cary today, with its richly-warm, ochre-coloured stone buildings, glows with good humour and benign sleepiness. The distinctive mediaeval-looking Market House, built to take advantage of the benefits the railway was to bring, used to echo with the turbulent voices of farmers and traders buying and selling butter and cheese, corn, meat and vegetables. It now accommodates the local museum, and though there is no longer a market day in the town, Castle Cary is still 'little', 'pleasant' and thriving.

The market place at Castle Cary in the early 1930s. The agricultural implements are arranged in the shade of the Market House.

Twenty-five miles to the north of Castle Cary is the city of Bath and due south, forty miles away, is the seaside town and harbour of Weymouth. The first railway built in Castle Cary parish was a cross-country line running between these two towns that still survives today, the Wilts, Somerset & Weymouth.

A cultural link between Bath and Weymouth had been established in the eighteenth century by Ralph Allen, entrepreneur, postman and quarrymaster. As a result of his influence and the whims of King George III, Bath and Weymouth were exploited as leisure resorts and became well patronised by the aristocracy. Both were also characterised by the local varieties of limestone which were quarried in the Bath area and at Portland. Georgian Bath was built of soft honeyed stone from the hills around the city, while sharp milk-white Portland stone had found its apotheosis the previous century when Wren had used it in building St Paul's. This geological connection gave rise to an industry which ultimately joined the two in name: the Bath & Portland Stone Firms Ltd of 1908.

Bath stone first travelled by rail at the bidding of Ralph Allen as early as 1731 from that gentleman's quarries high up on Combe Down, descending to the nether bank of the Avon at Bath. The distance was relatively short and the rails were wooden, but in thus operating one of the earliest railways in the south of England, Allen had sown a seed. The railway as a mode of transport thereafter took a hundred years to develop its grandest and most effective exposition, the seminal, inter-city, Liverpool & Manchester Railway. Engineered in the north country, refined by men of genius, the railway began to reach out across the countryside.

William IV was king. The Reform Act of 1832 reflected the broadening political awareness that was being stimulated by the new industrial age. The Poor Law of 1834 established the union workhouse, as if to repress the labouring people who were finding a voice to oppose the mechanisation which they saw threatening their livelihoods. The railway could bring fear and despair or the promise of work to those who lived by their hands. It could bring prosperity or ruin to those who created and directed wealth.

In 1835 the merchants of Bristol, riding the crest of a railway building wave, obtained an Act of Parliament for their Great Western Railway from London to Bristol. The prospectus upon which they raised the necessary finance described an offshoot from the main line at Corsham to serve the Wiltshire wool towns of Bradford and Trowbridge. It pointed temptingly towards the heart of Somerset and the following year an independent company, the Bath & Weymouth Great Western Union Railway, amplified this idea with a line that would have reached through Somerset and down to the Dorset coast. What traffic did the directors hope to carry on their line? Freestone from Bath? Portland stone from the coast? Agricultural produce, milk and cheese from the country areas? 'Cheap and abundant coals' from Radstock? Raw wool and finished textiles to and from the clothing districts? Ironstone from the Mendips? Fish? Travellers from Southern Ireland to the Channel Islands? Bewigged Rowlandsonesque characters with their gouty limbs propped up on the seats, journeying between salt-sea air and hot mineral-water springs for the good of their health?

The main line of this railway followed much of the route, and certainly presaged the ostensible purpose, of the later Wilts, Somerset & Weymouth Railway. It was surveyed by a Bath engineer called Roger Hopkins who claimed previous experience of railway construction in Cornwall.

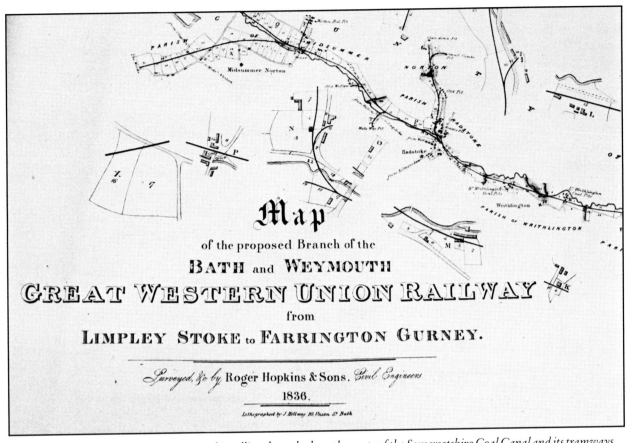

The deposited plan of the Bath & Weymouth's colliery branch along the route of the Somersetshire Coal Canal and its tramways.
S.R.O.

In fact, Hopkins had engineered the early and individualistic 'Dartmoor' gauge (4′ 6″) Plymouth & Dartmoor Railway, opened in 1823, and the distant but strategic Bodmin & Wadebridge Railway opened in 1834. The Bodmin & Wadebridge was Cornwall's first to be worked by steam locomotives, and was acquired by the London & South Western Railway in the mid-1840s, substantiating the L&SWR's desire to build a railway route to the far West. But both these Hopkins railways were fundamentally mineral lines, carrying granite and sand respectively.

His plan now was to fill all available interconnecting valleys to the south of Bath with single-track lines which snaked off in all directions at once, tapping the coalfields of North Somerset, the woollen towns and villages of the Avon valley and its tributaries, and finally of course the Royal watering place and Post Office packet station of Weymouth. It was ambitious and obviously drew its inspiration (in commercial if not engineering terms) from the Great Western Railway, construction of which was already firmly in progress. A similarly titled and ultimately more successful Great Western Union Railway to Cheltenham had been surveyed by Brunel and was destined for Parliament that summer. So the directors of the Bath & Weymouth, boosted by the glowing self-esteem of their engineer, were confident. Mr. Hopkins was so forcible and convincing 'that many who went to vote *against* the further progress of the undertaking, subsequently became its most strenuous supporters'.

The main line was planned via Frome, Witham, Wincanton, Stalbridge, Cerne Abbas and Dorchester. Two lines left Bath, one meandering, then as now, up the Avon valley, the other burrowing in an enormous tunnel under Combe Down to meet it near Monkton Combe. Colliery branches wandered up the valley of the Wellow brook to Radstock, and from Midford up the Cam valley to Timsbury. The main line, heading south, turned up the valley of the Frome

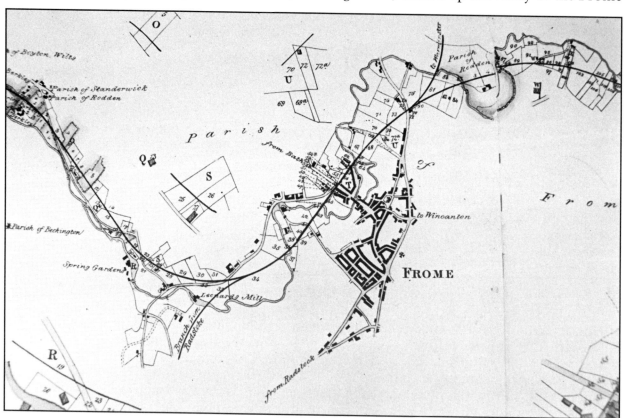

The route of the Bath & Weymouth up the Frome valley through the town.

S.R.O.

and wound through Farleigh Hungerford and Beckington to Frome itself. More branches continued up the Avon valley from Freshford to Bradford, and then up beside the Biss to Trowbridge, Westbury and Warminster. Cross lines linked Radstock, Frome and Warminster, a little branch ran off from Great Elm to Vobster and Coleford, and finally the main line rather uneventfully slunk down through Dorset to the sea. A separate Salisbury & Warminster Railway had been surveyed by Hopkins as an extension to the Bath & Weymouth but seems to have disappeared with little support.

The routes chosen echo those of the ill-fated Dorset & Somerset Canal, once planned to link the Kennet & Avon Canal and the collieries around Coleford with the south coast at Poole, and those of the Somersetshire Coal Canal, planned, built, prospering in the Somerset coalfield and now very upset by the Bath & Weymouth scheme. In fact in the mid-twenties two previous railway schemes had been attempted which became entangled in the death throes of the Dorset & Somerset Canal. These, the plain Western Railway and the self-explanatory Radstock, Shaftesbury & Poole, had made rather uncertain plans to connect the Bristol and English Channels, passing in the former case from west to east across the Cary lands and in the latter, from north to south between the towns of its title.

These lines had been promoted in the wake of the success of the Stockton & Darlington Railway and would have reflected the unsophisticated technology of the period. There is a suggestion that Messrs. Hopkins and Sons' current work also derived from that era of railway pre-history and took little account of the substantial advances in civil and mechanical engineering of the intervening years. The pit owners thought well of the Bath & Weymouth but the Somersetshire Coal Canal proprietors took up quantities of space in the press to attack it.

They tried to ridicule the estimated cost of building and running the line and the anticipated income from carrying coal. They pointed out that there was only one stage coach running through between Bath and Weymouth and that more people travelled from east to west than from north to south. There were actually a number of coaches. The *John Bull* and the *Wellington* made the patriotic double journey between the two towns three times a week in the forties, meeting usually at Bruton. A four-horse coach travelled the road between Bristol and Weymouth.

Roger Hopkins wrote in voluble reply to his critics that the Bath & Weymouth was 'different' from other railways. It was to be mostly single track, not many houses needed to be demolished, the value of the land required was low, stone blocks on which the iron rails would be mounted could be procured easily down the length of the line, 'in some places to be found adjoining the railway', and with a flourish he indicated 'the contiguity of the Cuttings to the Embankments, and the approximation of the one to the other' – a popular faux pas of the time!

When subjected to admittedly partisan scrutiny the railway began to look desperately unsound. Nevertheless, through what can only be regarded charitably as an oversight, the scheme proceeded to Parliament. Unknown to many of the directors, the capital had not been adequately subscribed so Mr. Hopkins had lopped off a few unnecessary branches to compensate. When the rejection by Parliament of the Bill at its second reading in May 1837 brought these strange occurrences to light, Captain George Scobell RN, a local director who had been on the committee of the earlier Radstock, Shaftesbury & Poole and whom we have not met for the last time, took command of a naturally heated exchange of views concerning the engineer and the solicitors. At a meeting of shareholders in the White Lion at Bath he summed up the whole saga by saying that he 'now looked upon this undertaking as dead and gone,' adding optimistically, 'its merits underrated'. And that would seem to have been the end of Messrs. Hopkins and Sons. The surveys, land plans and books of reference were filed away, and the idea of linking the Great Western with the south coast slept in dusty deed boxes for some eight years, during which period of fermentation a young queen ascended the throne and a new era began.

The idea was reawakened when the Great Western found its broad gauge monopoly of the West Country threatened by the extending tentacles of the ambitious but conventional South Western Railway. The Great Western had opened its main line in 1841 and pushed its magnificent empire westwards by way of lesser companies which paid tribute to itself. But in so doing, the intention to build the forked branch from Thingley to the Avon mill towns had been cast aside. In 1844 the paternal Great Western brought forth another sibling called the Wilts & Somerset Railway, which was essentially a version of that branch extended to the spiring city of Salisbury, with an eye towards the sea and the navy harboured at Portsmouth. Off-shoots led to the market towns of Devizes and Frome and beyond, to tap the fruits of the Somerset coalfield at Radstock. The company was transformed later that year into another bearing a longer title and with a prospectus enlarged accordingly, the Wilts, Somerset & Weymouth Railway.

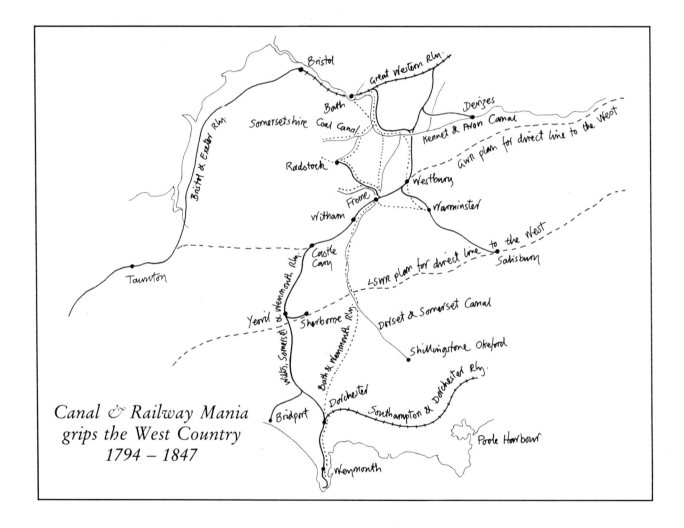

Canal & Railway Mania grips the West Country 1794 – 1847

Though promoted locally by an independent company, Brunel was present at the first meeting in Warminster and the Great Western was involved from the start. It was intended to build a line embodying all the chief proposals made so far by the original Great Western Act, the Bath & Weymouth, the Wilts & Somerset and the southern part of a lately abandoned Bristol & Exeter Railway scheme to join Taunton, Yeovil and Weymouth. In addition to the main line were branches leaving it at almost every other station. A local railway from Melksham to Devizes had been surveyed by Brunel for the grandly titled Melksham, Devizes & Great Western Union Railway in 1836, and now a similar one was inked on the map, together with others to Bradford, Radstock, Salisbury, Sherborne and Bridport, making a total of 148 miles of railway. The Bradford branch was later extended down the Avon Valley to Bathampton, but otherwise it was more or less the railway that exists today.

A major and significant difference between the Bath & Weymouth and the Wilts, Somerset & Weymouth routes could be observed in that area of high country which divides the north-flowing headwaters of the Avon tributaries from the west-flowing headwaters of the Brue and the King's Sedgemoor Drain. Whereas the Bath & Weymouth passed here through Witham along the same route as the Wilts, Somerset & Weymouth, it headed from north-east to south-west only so far as geographical convenience dictated a shift from a decisively north to south line. The Wilts, Somerset & Weymouth on the other hand extended this north-east to south-west axis for some eighteen miles from Westbury to Castle Cary. And for a very good reason.

In a world where the British lion stood without equal in the world, the adventurers of commercial capital were often characterised in military metaphors. So it may be observed, with contemporary precedent, that the Great Western was launching a two-pronged attack upon the South Western who were eagerly attempting to reach Exeter. The Great Western's strategy was not only to occupy the vital area of country through which any direct railway from London to the West would have to pass, but also for the distance that its railway of occupation ran fortuitously from north-east to south-west, to form part of just such a line. The Great Western was understandably worried that this direct railway, if not responsible to itself, would compete with its own circuitous route already in use by way of Bristol. This very good reason was further emphasised by subsequent Wilts, Somerset & Weymouth Acts of Parliament which altered the railway to be even more favourably aligned.

However, after some bickering between the two companies over certain other railways in disputed territory, they came to as amicable an arrangement as boardroom compromise would allow. They agreed to respect each other's areas of operation, whilst closing their eyes to each other's overt designs on a direct route to the West Country. It was inevitably only a temporary peace, paid for by the loss of the strange Southampton & Dorchester to the South Western, but at least the Wilts, Somerset & Weymouth was assured of an easy passage through Parliament. Its passage through King Arthur's Country was not so easily bought.

'Here the grass was thick, rich and succulent, and a dark shade of green which contrasted with the molten-silver of the railway line running straight into the evening sun'.   The Chronicles of Church Farm, South Barrow – *Monica Hutchings*

Looking south west towards the tree-lined borders of William Brown's fields in the distance.

2
*F*ARMER *B*ROWN

Just to the south of Castle Cary, close to the village of North Barrow, lies a spread of pasture owned in the mid-1840s by a certain Somerset yeoman whose name was William Brown. He was, we may be sure, a worldly and respectable farmer whose grazing was as lush as any in the district. He lived at North Barrow with his wife Ann and his daughter Mary. He was advancing in years but was probably still working the land which had been altered so little by the passing centuries. At about this time however, there began a twelve year period of procrastination and obduracy which eventually brought about a change to the Cary lands. The surveyors of the Wilts, Somerset & Weymouth, with Brunel at their head, had determined that their railway, heading southwards from Frome towards the market town of Yeovil, should furrow across these lands like the weal of a giant plough. The local people first felt this relentless omnipotence in the form of convoluted legal documents, some barely understandable by speakers of the common tongue, borne to them by the recently established penny post.

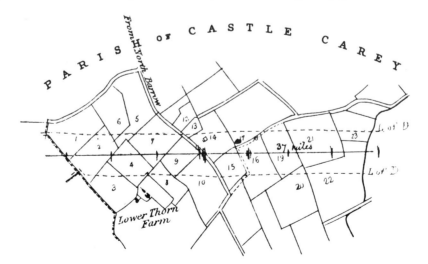

From the deposited plans of the Wilts, Somerset & Weymouth Railway, showing the line across William Brown's land, 1844.

S.R.O.

In December 1844 Farmer Brown received a printed letter signed by Harry Russ, a prominent Castle Cary solicitor, reciting a list of towns to be served by the proposed railway, and giving a detailed description of those parts of Mr Brown's property it would cross, together with a plan. Finally it requested him to indicate 'whether you assent or dissent from the proposed undertaking, or whether you are neuter in respect thereto'. Recommendation from the landowners would be invaluable support for the company's application to Parliament, but we have no record of Mr Brown's reply. He would probably have had nothing to gain by opposing it.

It was intended that the railway should carry itself upon a low embankment, about four or five feet high, across Mr Brown's fields. Immediately northward of them, the road from North Barrow to Galhampton crosses the line of the railway. To the west runs the Barrow brook, a tributary of the Cary, marking the parish boundary, and beyond on gently rising ground is North Barrow. It is probably little bigger today than it was then or at Domesday when it was first recorded. Not a pretty village, but a practical one of solid houses with thick grey and ochre stone walls, surrounded by flat green fields and flattering apple orchards. The minute church of St. Nicholas, almost dwarfed by its attendant yew and concealed at the head of the village, is probably more changed than the farmhouses, having been rebuilt and restored by Victorian benefactors.

Apple trees and cows at North Barrow. The parish boundary follows the Barrow brook which passes under the road at this point. The farm house is actually in Castle Cary parish.

Wilts, Somerset, and Weymouth Railway.

CASTLE CARY, 1st December, 1844.

Sir,

I beg to inform you, that Application is intended to be made to Parliament in the ensuing Session, for an Act to authorise the formation of a Railway or Railways, with Branches from the Great Western Railway, near Corsham, to the Towns of Melksham, Devizes, Bradford, Trowbridge, Westbury, Frome, Radstock, Warminster, Salisbury, Sherborne, Yeovil, Bridport, Dorchester and Weymouth, and that the Property mentioned in the annexed Schedule, or some part thereof, in which I understand you are interested as therein stated, will or may be required for the purposes of the said Undertaking according to the Line thereof, as at present laid out, or under the usual powers of deviation therefrom, or of alteration of the said Line, which will be applied for in the intended Act to such extent as is shown on the Plans hereinafter mentioned, and will (if the said Line as at present laid out be adopted) be passed through in the manner mentioned in such Schedule.

I also beg to inform you, that a Plan and Section of the said Undertaking, with a Book of Reference thereto, were deposited for public inspection with the Clerks of the Peace of the Counties of Wilts, Somerset, and Dorset respectively, and of the City of New Sarum, on the 30th of November last, and that a Copy of so much of the said Plan, Section, and Book of Reference as relates to the Parish in which your Property is situate, will be deposited for public inspection with the Clerk of the said Parish, on or before the 31st day of December instant, on which Plans respectively your Property will appear designated by the numbers set forth in the annexed Schedule.

As I am required to report to Parliament whether you assent to or dissent from the proposed Undertaking, or whether you are neuter in respect thereto, you will oblige me by writing your answer of assent, dissent, or neutrality, in the form left herewith, and returning the same to me with your signature on or before the 10th day of January next; and if there should be any error or mis-description in the annexed Schedule, I shall feel obliged by your informing me thereof, at your earliest convenience, that I may correct the same without delay.

I am,

Your most obedient Servant,

HARRY RUSS.

To

Mr. William Brown
Castle Cary

WILTS, SOMERSET, AND WEYMOUTH RAILWAY.

PLAN OF PROPERTY IN THE PARISH OF

Castle Carey

BELONGING TO

William Brown

CONTAINING   A.   R.   P.   1 .. 2 .. 26

SCALE, FOUR CHAINS TO ONE INCH.

   The area of land required by the railway was just over an acre, and what remained of the
fields would naturally be reduced in size and split up, being considerably devalued as a result.
Rights of access between two of the fields would be threatened and a small watercourse which
dribbled along their common boundary across the path of the line would have to be accom-
modated. The surviving land plan, shown opposite, is copiously annotated in the pencilled hand
of Mr. Brown's attorney, a land agent from Bruton called Bennett. It shows in black ink three
fields or closes, and in red the line of the railway, cutting across them. One field which is
marked 'arable and brook' loses a small part in a corner, another marked 'pasture and shed' or
'stall' is struck right through the middle into two, and the third marked 'pasture' loses a large
corner segment. The neighbouring fields have been pencilled in, and also shown in this way are
the Barrow brook with the watercourse feeding into it, a public footpath heading over the
largest, central field towards North and South Cadbury, a private road leading into an
adjoining field of Mr. Brown's called the Dry Close, and the public highway mentioned
previously, marked 'rail to go under the road'. The sketch indicates how the line of the road
would have to be kinked to avoid crossing the railway at too sharp an angle. The pathways are
shown in wiggling lines or small dashes, and little gates are drawn at the points where they enter
the various fields.
   The notes rough out some ideas for overcoming the inconveniences caused by the railway,
which would have involved buying up nearby fields: 'Bennett's road to be got rid of' (not the
same Bennett). 'Buy up Mr. Danbury's 8 Acres and if not, must have a direct road access by the
stall. If he cannot get Mr. Danbury's rough ground by purchase exchange Dry Close for it.' The
railway was going to sever William Brown's access from the road to those fields which would
lie on the far or east side of the line. His best plan was to buy Mr. Danbury's adjoining 8-acre
field across which he had a right of way to these fields. This would rationalise the oddly-shaped
remnants and the access to them. Failing purchase, he would need a new road across the railway
near the stall in field No 2. Mr. Brown was evidently willing to exchange his arable Dry Close
for Mr. Danbury's field if he could not purchase it. He was obviously in a position to buy up
his neighbours' fields in preference to selling off his severed pieces.
   This effect of the railway interestingly echoes the problems brought about by enclosure in
the seventeenth and eighteenth centuries, when small open fields scattered about the parish were
often swapped around between their tenants in order to form enclosed fields of a sensible size
and shape.
   Today William Brown's fields can be surveyed from the railway overbridge. The stretch of
line between Castle Cary and Sparkford runs almost dead straight and level, arrowing nearly
from horizon to horizon across a broad vista of greens, cobalt, emerald, viridian and olive,
which extends from the distant bluish ramparts of Cadbury Castle in the south-east to the pale
misty merging of heaven and earth in the farmost west. The boundary hedges of road, railway
and field are thick and full grown. Tall, mature beeches and oaks are loosely ranked in the
hedgerows. A single tree stands alone in the middle of a field where perhaps a hedge has been
grubbed up. A small group of heifers ruminates beside a gate. Careful scrutiny of the scruffy
ground beside the bridge, and reference to a large scale Ordnance Survey map clearly show how
the road at this vantage point was reconstructed when the railway was built, rising up on a new
line from the level of the fields, gaining sufficient height to leap over the railway on its solid but

elegant grey stone bridge. Occasionally a rumbling rattle stirs up on the breeze and a diesel multiple unit looms and sways into view. The Weymouth train glides past leaving a small diffuse cærulean fog hanging in the sparkling air.

3

VERY USEFUL & COMPLETE

During the Parliamentary session of 1845 the Wilts, Somerset & Weymouth Bill was debated and, with none of the prevarication of the coming years and with only a hint of reluctance, it was accorded the Royal Assent. The Lords required only an assurance from the promoters that 'the extension of the line to Weymouth shall not be set up hereafter to defeat a direct line from London to Falmouth'.

'We want to have the red line,' said my Lord Cadogan, 'and we hesitate to grant you this Wilts, Somerset & Weymouth line, because we fear that one day or other you will set this line up in opposition to the central line of which we see the necessity...' Nevertheless it was done.

Lord Dalhousie's Board of Trade report earlier that year observed that the South Western had already withdrawn its proposals (the 'central line'), made in opposition to the Great Western, and went on to commend the Wilts, Somerset & Weymouth scheme which, together with the Bristol & Exeter's Yeovil branch, 'form a comprehensive system of North and South communication'. The South Western plan for a shorter route from London to the West was thought to be less favourable in view of the local connections afforded by the Wilts, Somerset & Weymouth, especially in the direction of Bristol and Bath to which cities a large quantity of traffic already made its way. 'A very useful and complete scheme for the accommodation of the district', waffled the report. The Chamber of Commerce in Bristol and other public bodies however, had expressed their wish for a direct line either by way of Radstock to Bristol or from Bradford to Bath along the Avon valley, as the promised route by way of Thingley was 'circuitous and imperfect'. In addition, the fact that the city of Wells had been ignored altogether was felt by the good Lord to have been a wanton omission. Indeed the Great Western must have had friends in high places even then, for its true motives were ill-concealed. E.T. MacDermot records that Saunders, the Great Western's secretary, told the Gauge Commissioners in 1846 that the Wilts, Somerset & Weymouth was *always* intended to form part of a direct line to Exeter, and this they were now plainly contemplating.

"Lord Kenyon, in his simplicity, thought they had bound the Great Western… You might as well soap your fingers and then try to hold an eel as expect to be able to bind down these gentlemen…"

Both companies subsequently rejoined the fight for the direct line to the west, and the celebrated, anti-climactic fifty-three day Parliamentary Committee hearing in the summer of 1847 ensured that, by giving both sides a slice of the cake, there were no winners, only sore heads, empty pockets and not a few regrets. "If the South Western had persisted in their opposition to the Wilts, Somerset & Weymouth, that line would not now be in existence" mourned the South Western counsel. If only!

The Battle of the Gauges, which is what lay behind this rivalry, was a sometimes fanatical confrontation of well-matched but incompatible principles, of radical creative engineering against the status quo, of Brunel's masterful broad gauge against the more manageable and prolific narrow gauge. It might seem strange that the measured distance between the rails on which the trains ran should have given rise to such a commotion, but it was a rather fundamental debate. It was a cut-throat economic conflict joined by powerful capitalistic interests, and the face of the land was to change dramatically over the next few decades, none of these altered aspects being so characteristic as the engineering works which graced the several railway companies' projects. Brunel had built the Great Western and left his distinctive autograph upon the swathe of countryside through which it passed. The way was now clear for his remarkable but already doomed broad gauge to reach southwards for the Channel, and occupy south-east Somerset.

In June 1846 Farmer Brown received a bluish document entitled "Notice to Deliver Particulars of Claim". In it the Wilts, Somerset & Weymouth declared that, under the powers of their Act, his land would be 'wanted and required for the purposes of the said Undertaking'. He was given twenty-one days in which to deliver a claim for compensation to their office at Trowbridge.

At this point we turn to Bennett's calculations, shrewdly committed in pencil to produce a negotiable but presentable sum on Mr. Brown's behalf. His notebook bound in limp, faded russet pigskin, contains details of nineteen local landowners and their property which was to be compulsorily purchased for the railway.

Page 52 begins: 'Mr. William Brown, Castle Cary, Tenant in Fee, Parts of 3 Closes'. The land, comprising one acre, two roods and twenty-six perches, Bennett values at £108 4s 6d. For the compulsory nature of the transaction he adds fifty per cent, £54 2s 3d. He then moves on to compensation and under the heading "Severance" notes: 'Separates a Meadow diagonally depriving one part of the use of a Stall and makes 2 other fields ill-shaped. Condition for an occupation Road and a Culvert for a Water Course in [field] No 4.' For this he adds £100. For loss of rent at 4/3d an acre he calculates 11 guineas and Land Tax at £5. Under the heading "Timber" he notes that a guinea's worth of ash trees would be lost from the middle field No 2, and under the mysterious heading "Damage to Tenant last year" he notes £50 'for loss of road'. Was this the consequence of heavy-footed surveyors at work? A quick addition gives us £329 18s 9d which Bennett rounds up nicely to £330 exclusive of expenses. The claim was posted off on July 18th and though a deal was apparently struck with no acrimony, six months passed before the Purchase Agreement was signed.

Mr William Brown   Castlesary

     Tenant in Fee   Two Rent charges ,4/3, p^r acre

              Land Tax £2.14.3 on whole Estate abo.^t 41½ acres

Parts of 3 Closes, viz

N.º 1 in Railway Plan - Worthy _ d   a r p

2 _ " _____ _ D.^o _ M   } 1. 2. 22 mg/ _ 3. 5. 6

4 ___ " _____ _ Thorn _ M

         Compulsory Sale 50 per Cent _ _ _ _ _ _

        Compensation

      Severance _ _ _ _ _ _ _ _ _ _   say _ _ _ _ _

separates a Meadow diagonally

depriving one part of the use of Stall

and makes 2 other fields ill shaped _

     Condition for an occupation Road

and a Culvert for Watercourse in N.º 4 _

     Would not like to sell severed parts

but would purchase rather _

     Rent charge _ 1. 2 22 at 4/3 _ 7/ at 83 _ _ _ _

     Land Tax _   say £3 P.a

     Timber _ _ _ _ _ _ _ _

     Expenses _

     Damage to Tenant last year

The land surveyor of the Wilts, Somerset & Weymouth was Giles Westbury of Andover. He formally agreed a price of £315 on January 29th 1847 'for the purchase of the Freehold and Inheritance in Fee-Simple of and all those pieces of land, containing one acre, two roods and twenty six Perches with Mines thereunder, and Timber thereon', the mines being purely figments of the legal mind. The usual expenses were to be borne by the company as was the cost of constructing 'a convenient crossing over the said railway to connect the Fields numbered 2 and 4' and the preservation of the watercourse between these fields. The railway track was to run a few feet above the level of the fields so a culvert would have posed no problem, but the nature of the crossing is not revealed in detail.

Inspection of the large-scale Ordnance Survey map opposite shows the watercourse following the shape of the original field even though that part of that particular field (the corner of field No 4) had been joined by then on to its larger neighbour. This strange wiggle has since been straightened out. The stall marked on the plan is still there, a rough low stone building with a terracotta pantile roof, still used for storing hay and still squatting imperturbably among the willows and the cows.

William Brown's fields today seen from the railway line.

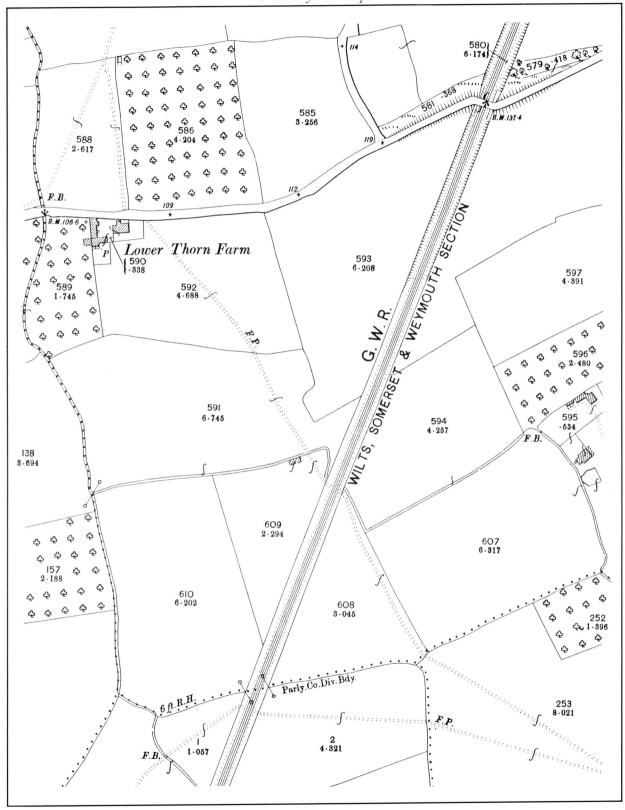

Lower Thorn Farm

G.W.R.

WILTS, SOMERSET & WEYMOUTH SECTION

588
2·617

586
4·204

585
3·256

580
6·174

579   ·418

581   ·368

B.M.137·4

119

114

112

109

F.B.

B.M.106·6

P

590
·338

589
1·745

592
4·688

593
6·208

597
4·391

596
2·480

595
·534

F.B.

591
6·745

594
4·257

F.P.

138
3·694

609
2·294

607
6·317

157
2·188

610
6·202

608
3·045

252
1·396

253
8·021

Parly. Co. Div. Bdy.

6 ft. R.H.

F.P.

F.B.

2
4·321

1·057

Above – Cows crossing the line near North Barrow in the sunshine of an autumn afternoon. Rev. R. Simmons
Opposite – Above is the sturdy stonework of the bridge carrying the North Barrow to Galhampton road
over the railway. Below – a diesel multiple unit passes under the bridge and heads across Farmer Brown's
fields for Yeovil, 1986.

Although there are a number of occupation farm crossings along this stretch of line, the one agreed with William Brown does not exist today. A slight flattening of the long grass and a pair of short fences which might once have been gates or stiles betray the site of this footpath crossing, but the railway makes no concession to it. Studying the lie of the land reveals some change in the shapes of the fields. Those immediately east of the railway (including field No 4) have lost their dividing boundaries and melded into a large meadow. Those to the west however have altered less. Between Brown's fields and the overbridge, the railway earthworks change imperceptibly from a slight embankment to a slight cutting. At the imperceptible join is a small cluster of semi-derelict platelayers' cabins, and a yellow painted milepost marking 132½ miles from Paddington.

Opening of the
WILTS & SOMERSET RAILWAY,

For the Conveyance of Passengers, Carriages, Horses, Goods, and Cattle.

On & after Tuesday, 5th September, 1848,
THE FOLLOWING TRAINS WILL RUN BETWEEN

Westbury and Chippenham,
CALLING AT THE INTERMEDIATE STATIONS, AT

TROWBRIDGE & MELKSHAM,
AND IN CONNEXION WITH THE "LONG" TRAINS OF THE

GREAT WESTERN RAILWAY.

UP.

Leaving Westbury	Trowbridge	Melksham	Arriving at Chippenham	In time for the
Class				
1st a.m.	a.m.	a.m.	a.m.	6.50 a.m. Up Express Train from Exeter.
2nd 8 10	8 19	8 24	8 40	8.5 Day Mail from Bristol.
3rd				7.10 Up Third Class Train from Bristol.
				9.40 a.m. Down Train from Paddington.
1st				8. 0 a.m. Up Train from Exeter.
2nd 10 45	10 57	11 12	11 30	6.55 Up Third Class Train from Exeter.
3rd				9.50 Down Express Train from Paddington.
1st p.m.	p.m.	p.m.	p.m.	12. 0 Up Express Train from Exeter.
2nd 1 30	1 39	1 51	2 5	12. 0 Down Train from Paddington.
1st				1. 0 Up Train from Exeter.
2nd 3 50	4 2	4 17	4 35	2. 0 Down Train from Paddington.
1st				3.15 p.m. Up Train from Exeter.
2nd 6 5	6 17	6 32	6 50	5.30 p.m. Down Express Train from Paddington.

DOWN.

Leaving Chippenham.	Melksham.	Trowbridge.	Arriving at Westbury.	Taking from the
Class				
1st a.m.	a.m.	a.m.	a.m.	6.50 Up Express Train from Exeter.
2nd 9 0	9 18	9 33	9 45	9. 0 Day Train from Paddington.
1st 11 50	12 6	12 20	12 30	8. 0 a.m. Up Train from Exeter.
2nd				9.50 Down Express Train from Paddington.
1st p.m.	p.m.	p.m.	p.m.	Down Day Mail from Paddington.
2nd 2 15	2 33	2 48	3 0	7. 5 Down Third Class Train from Paddington.
3rd				6.55 Up Third Class Train from Exeter.
1st				1. 0 p.m. Up Train from Exeter.
2nd 5 5	5 23	5 58	5 50	2. 0 p.m. Down Train from Paddington.
3rd				11.50 a.m. Down Train Third Class from Paddington.
1st 7 40	7 56	8 10	8 20	5.30 p.m. Down Express Train from Paddington.
2nd				3.15 p.m. Up Train from Exeter.

SUNDAYS.

Class	a.m.	a.m.	a.m.	a.m.	
1st					8.45 Down Train from Swindon.
2nd 8 35	8 47	9 2	9 20	10.15 Down Train from Paddington.
3rd				8.45 Up Train from Bristol.
				6.35 Up Train from Exeter.
1st p.m.	p.m.	p.m.	p.m.	2. 0 Down Train from Paddington.
2nd 3 53	4 5	4 20	4 38	1. 0 Up Train from Exeter.
3rd				

SUNDAYS.

Class	a.m.	a.m.	a.m.	p.m.	
1st					8.35 Up Train from Bristol.
2nd 9 40	9 58	10 13	10 25	8.45 Down Train from Swindon.
3rd				
1st p.m.	p.m.	p.m.	p.m.	6.35 Up Train from Exeter.
2nd 5 45	6 3	6 18	6 30	1. 0 Up Train from Exeter.
3rd				7.15 Down Train from Paddington.
				10.15 Down Train from Paddington.
				2. 0 Down Train from Paddington.

FARES.

FROM WESTBURY TO	EXPRESS. 1st Class.	EXPRESS. 2nd Class.	ORDINARY TRAIN. 1st Class.	ORDINARY TRAIN. 2nd Class.	ORDINARY TRAIN. 3rd Class.	CARRIAGES. 4-wheel.	CARRIAGES. 2-wheel.	HORSES. Each.	HORSES. Per Pair.
	s. d.	s. d.	s. d.	s. d.	s. d.	s. d.	s. d.	s. d.	s. d.
Trowbridge	—	—	1 3	0 9	0 4	8 0	6 0	7 0	12 0
Melksham	—	—	2 6	1 6	0 9	9 0	7 0	8 0	13 0
Chippenham	—	—	3 6	2 0	1 3	11 0	8 0	9 0	14 0
Bath	4 6	3 0	4 0	2 6	1 10	12 0	9 0	10 0	15 0
Bristol	7 0	4 6	6 6	4 0	2 9	16 0	13 0	14 0	20 0
Paddington	28 0	19 6	25 0	16 6	9 0	56 0	45 0	50 0	70 0

An additional Fare will be charged for the *Express Trains* between *Chippenham* and all other Stations.

For further particulars see the General Time Tables.

5th September, 1848.

4

*A P*ERFECT *B*UBBLE

Things were moving slowly in Castle Cary. But further up the line the solicitors, surveyors, engineers, navvies and platelayers had been working with slightly more urgency on the construction of the railway from Thingley, west of Chippenham on the Great Western main line, as far as Westbury. On Tuesday September 5th 1848 the first temporary wooden terminus of the Wilts, Somerset & Weymouth was opened, still embarrassingly located in Wiltshire, just short of the border. The previous Saturday had been junketing day for the directors. With Daniel Gooch and Brunel upon the footplate of *Vulture*, a special train ran from Thingley calling first at Melksham for 'loud cheering' and 'flag waving', then at Trowbridge for 'salutes of cannon' and finally arriving at Westbury for a 'congratulatory address' from the Mayor. They all returned to Melksham for a 'déjeuner à la fourchette' in the Town Hall. The new line was leased to the Great Western who provided the locomotives and carriages with which to operate a service. This right had been secured by the Great Western agreeing to guarantee minimum divided payments to shareholders.

At the Westbury terminus, passengers and trains were protected by a large wooden roof which spanned the tracks and platforms. The intermediate stations at Melksham and at Trowbridge, where the company's offices were situated, had been built of stone in the manner of the solid Tudoresque designs originally conceived by Brunel for the Great Western. So the hand of the true progenitors of the local line was visible to any who closely studied the new structures.

A railhead had been established, but the Wilts, Somerset & Weymouth had struggled so far to build fourteen miles of double track railway, and would struggle no further. The company had run out of money and the whole country was now gripped by a stringent reaction to the speculative rash of the Mania years. The early forties had seen general prosperity and a tendency to overproduce. This had fuelled the urge to speculate: Parliament had faced over a thousand railway bills in 1845. Successful railways stimulated the economy even more, but inevitably towards the end of 1847 crisis struck. Banks failed. Businesses were ruined. In a few months revolution would break out in Paris. The marathon Parliamentary Committee hearing that summer had presided over a riot of Channel to Channel and east to west railway proposals. The Wilts, Somerset & Weymouth had limped into the fray with one of each, the Bleadon to Blandford and the Compton to Wilton lines. But the poorly finances of the company had even then been obvious to the opposition.

The perfection of country station design photographed around the turn of the century. Solid, secure, almost ecclesiastical, Melksham station awaits its passengers. The goods shed to the left was built in the same style. Note that the up line, though narrowed, is still laid with broad gauge bridge-rail on longitudinal timbers.

'Now!' shouts Mr. Cockburn, presenting the South Western's case to the Committee, 'I undertake to demonstrate that there is not the remotest possibility of their constructing the line…here not a single part, from one end to the other, of the Wilts, Somerset & Weymouth line has either been opened, or is now in a state of such forwardness as will enable them to hold out…the least expectation that it will be opened in reasonable time. Now!' he repeats, 'with regard to the three branches [Devizes, Sherborne and Bridport], they have not taken one single step towards the construction of them…and it appears they are not even contracted for.' He points to the undersubscribed capital and the obvious financial strings binding the company to the Great Western.

'A man may purchase now at £10 shares upon which £20 has been paid… I ask, will any man of common sense pretend to say that it will be in the power of the Company to get their calls responded to, and their capital paid up, so as to construct these works? It is clear that their condition is absolutely hopeless…

'The Wilts, Somerset & Weymouth subscription contract is signed not by the Wilts, Somerset & Weymouth Company but by the Great Western on behalf of the Wilts, Somerset & Weymouth Company. According to the terms of the bill they are to have the *power* of making the line without being under any *obligation* to do so.'

He chides the Wilts, Somerset & Weymouth for borrowing illegally from the Great Western and the Great Western for borrowing illegally from the open market. 'It cannot legally borrow; nevertheless it does so. It wants to come to Parliament this year…It has not money wherewith to construct the works; it has not even wherewith to pay the deposits. It would be idle to issue shares in the Compton and Wilton line. There is not a man who woud not turn up his nose at them. But the Great Western are extremely anxious to cover the country, and where is the money to be found? Like their neighbours of the Wilts, Somerset & Weymouth they were a little out at [the] elbows and the only mode in which they could find the money was by borrowing…' and with a grand gesture the orator despatches all things Great and Western, 'Upon this, Sir, I say the whole thing is a perfect bubble.' And so it was.

In 1846 the Great Western had failed to achieve a direct line to the West by way of Hungerford, Westbury and Yeovil. In 1847 the 'perfect bubble' had burst. It was not long before the Great Western decided to come clean over its involvement with the Wilts, Somerset & Weymouth, and absorb its protégé altogether on March 14th 1850. Building work had been proceeding on the next section of line and later that year the railway crossed at last into Somerset with a new temporary timber terminus at Frome which is still in use today, well restored with a grant, and a commemorative plaque. The Salisbury branch was similarly opened as far as Warminster the following year, with a terminus not unlike that at Frome, but not destined to last so long.

Once again, however, enthusiasm for the project seemed to flag. Direct broad and narrow gauge lines to the West Country had been authorised by Parliament in 1848 but no-one could afford to build them. By entering a ridiculous scheme (the Wilts, Somerset & Weymouth bubble – an 'unnecessary and mischievous' line) and a reasonably sound one (the Berks & Hants Extension Railway from Hungerford to Westbury together with a Bristol & Exeter Railway line from Durston to Castle Cary, approved by the Commons in 1847 and the Lords the following year), the Great Western had hedged its bets. So both contestants had won the battle but both

Great Western Railway. Wilts & Somerset Ry

Trowbridge ~~STATION.~~

5 October 1852

Dear Sir,

I beg to acknowledge receipt of your favor of yesterdays date the delay you complain of has arisen from the desire Mr Ward had first to consult Mr Brunel (who until the last few days has been out of England) as to some gradients — Mr Ward is now in London for that purpose and so far as I am concerned I do not see any reason why your purchase may not be settled by the end of next week — I shall be in Salisbury to morrow and Thursday — after which I will get Mr Ward to appoint the day to be at Bruton — will you have the goodness to assure Mr Bennett from me that the above is the reason of the delay

Yrs faithfully

Richard Jarr

J Balch Esqr
Bruton

had lost the war. The Great Western had marked out its territory and was now content to allow the various earthworks and other preparations down the length of the unopened Weymouth line to lie abandoned. Indeed the notorious case of Bradford-on-Avon, which possessed a fine Cotswold stone station building virtually completed by the Wilts, Somerset & Weymouth company, illustrates the want of concern on the part of the Great Western. For Bradford's cloth trade had declined severely since the branch line had been proposed originally and the tracks to the town remained unlaid for nearly ten years. Naturally money was at the root of this half-heartedness, and one of the shortest-lived railway companies was now launched in a spiritless attempt to raise public support for the line. The Frome, Yeovil & Weymouth Railway existed in theory for three months during 1852 with the object of completing the unfinished railway, but with no assets save its Westminster address. When this paper railway folded, the Great Western was left once again holding the baby.

Eventually things picked up. The grand and fanciful Great Exhibition of 1851 had helped to ease the seized wheels of the economy, and slowly confidence was restored in the railway systems which now enwebbed the country. Work began again along the course of the Wilts, Somerset & Weymouth urged on by public complaint and the serving of writs, notably in connection with the Limpley Stoke valley and Devizes branches. Deals were completed for parcels of land, which had been left in abeyance. Stations and bridges were constructed. Rails were laid.

At the end of August 1856 the *Western Flying Post* reported warily on the suggestion that the next part of the line was ready. 'In answer to numerous inquiries as to the day when the Wilts, Somerset & Weymouth Railway will be opened? We can only answer in the trite old saying that "seeing is believing". We have been told that the section from Frome to Yeovil would be open in ten days. This has been the floating report for nearly a month. Railway directors are the only persons who reckon time after the Oriental fashion, like the salutation "may you live for ever", ten days means nothing more than some *railway* indefinite period of time, it may mean a month, it may mean more than a month, but certainly not ten days.' And the prognosis for the final run to the sea was regarded with similar cynicism. A letter from the Great Western was produced: '…every exertion…earliest possible completion…Mr. Brunel personally on the line to assist in accelerating the work…' and so on.

GREAT WESTERN RAILWAY.

NOTICE is hereby given, that, on MONDAY, the 1st of SEPTEMBER, the WILTS and SOMERSET BRANCH of the Great Western Railway was OPENED to YEOVIL, for the conveyance of passengers, parcels, carriages, and horses.

For particulars of trains see the Company's time bill, to be obtained at the Paddington Station, and at the booking offices.

Paddington, August 28, 1856.

Western Flying Post

Sparkford station c1905. North Barrow village lies a couple of miles beyond the trees, actually closer to this than to Castle Cary station.

But it was now twelve years since the route had been surveyed by the Wilts, Somerset & Weymouth, and at last the alterations to Mr. Brown's three fields at Castle Cary were beginning to take on the appearance of a railway. He might have been watching at around 7 o'clock in the morning on Monday September 1st 1856 as the glinting brasswork, hot green paint and whispering steam of a Great Western locomotive headed, clattering, out across the fields on a single broad gauge track from Sparkford station with the first trainload of passengers for Castle Cary and Frome. The machine that was changing the face of the land and the pulse of its life was arriving in the heart of Somerset. Sadly however, William Brown did not see it. He had been born in the Georgian era and lived through times of great turmoil, but he did not live to see the railway arrive at his doorstep. He had been buried in the secluded peace of North Barrow churchyard on July 8th 1853 aged 76, and the railway passed him by.

Harry Russ too had died a couple of years before the line opened. He was the Cary solicitor who had acted on behalf of the Wilts, Somerset & Weymouth. His successor, his nephew Charles, was secretary and treasurer of a company set up to build a new Market House in Castle Cary. The anticipated completion of the railway had given considerable impetus to this plan and the House had been opened just in time. The Wilts, Somerset & Weymouth had arrived, and the area would prosper on its account. Henceforth milk was whisked away to the large towns and

Castle Cary station photographed on May 20th 1922 by J. B. Sherlock.

CASTLE CARY
GREAT CHEESE MARKETS.

OPENING of the WILTS and SOMERSET RAILWAY to CASTLE CARY.

TO CHEESE FACTORS AND OTHERS.

A Great Number of the Principal Dairy Proprietors in the Neighbourhood of CASTLE CARY having agreed to PITCH CHEESE at the MARKETS, which will be held on September 30th, October 28th, and November 25th, the following PRIZES will be given on Sept. 30th:—

For the largest quantity of Cheese, of not less than £ three tons, the produce of the same Dairy, pitched by the producer 3

For the best lot of Cheese, not less than 30 cwt., pitched by the producer 2

For the best lot of truckle Cheese, not less than 5 cwt., pitched by the producer 1

CHARLES RUSS, Hon. Sec.
Castle Cary, 8th September, 1856.

Bath Chronicle

new, more efficient farming equipment arrived by train. Whereas other country areas, particularly the neighbouring chalk lands to the south, suffered in subsequent years at the hands of the newcomer from the import of foreign wheat, the claylands flourished. Prizes were offered for cheese. Milk churns stood in dozens on the local station platform.

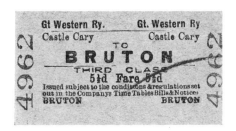

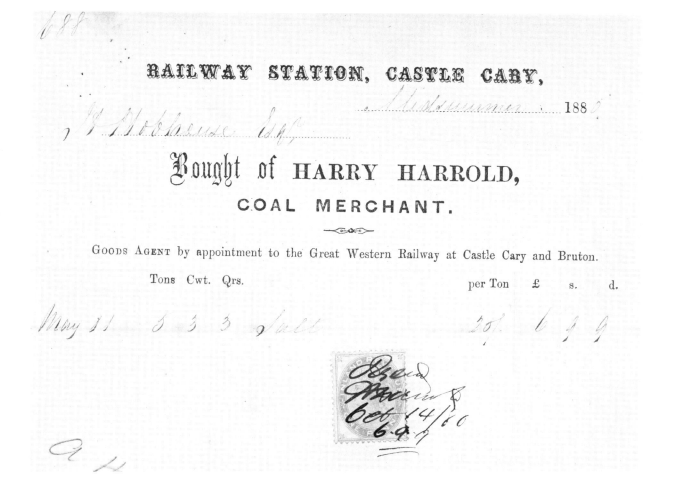

The railway crossed into Dorset the following year when it opened in its entire length to a final and permanent wooden-roofed terminus at Weymouth. It had cost the Broad Gauge £1½ million and taken twenty years to reach the Channel haven.

Witham station c1905. By this time it had become a junction for the East Somerset line to Wells. The passenger luggage labels, below, probably date from the opening of the railway in 1856.

GWR
Maiden Newton to
Witham

GWR
Westbury to
Marston

PART 2

Ludlows Colliery, Radstock in the 1930s. The pit first wound coal c1784, and was closed in 1954.

5

A Waggonful of Bullocks

In the great Parliamentary inquiry which set out during 1847 to referee the Battle of Castle Cary for the main line to the West, Mr. Cockburn, whom we have already met, accused the Great Western of putting up lines purely to occupy territory and mark out boundaries, rather than to serve communities and carry their traffic, of ignoring local people, setting out merely to 'abridge the distance between the terminal points' and of sacrificing 'the whole of Somerset to that object'.

'They begin', he declared, 'with twenty witnesses from the top of their crossline between Bleadon and Wells, the greater part of whom I do not believe had ever heard of Dorset – certainly not been through it; many had not heard of Bruton. They had been buried in that happy cheese-growing country of Cheddar and probably had never been out of it. Others had heard of Bruton, but had never seen it.'

He continued in this incisive and caustic style to suggest that this 'cheese-growing country', the local assize towns, the manufacturing and county towns deserved better attention to their real needs. 'What should have prevented them, instead of running their line from Castle Cary to Taunton, from taking their line from Frome by Shepton Mallet, Wells, Glastonbury and Bridgewater? It would be quite as short…' he addressed the committee, '…should you not pause and take care, lest in sanctioning the Castle Cary line you do not present an obstacle to the construction of a future line which would afford *real* accommodation to this district.

'That there ought to be a line through that central part of Somersetshire – that there must be a line from Bridgewater to Glastonbury, and from Glastonbury to Wells, and from Wells to Shepton Mallet, and from Shepton Mallet to Frome, connecting itself with the broad gauge line to London – no man can doubt.'

Here was wisdom indeed! Such lines were built in the end, of course, but by local companies, too late to bring major economic growth to the area, and thereby fated to perish in the 1960s with so many others.

As to the broad gauge, Mr. Cockburn mocked the Great Western and their attempts to gloss over the obstacles presented at certain stations to traffic transferring from wagons of one gauge to those of another. He quoted their offer; 'we shall give you advantages which will be more than equivalent to all the inconveniences you may sustain, because…' and Mr. Cockburn's scornful glance can be well imagined at this point, 'because we shall bring you the *coal of Radstock*. This is the great case that has been made on the part of the Great Western to show that this district [the Wiltshire, Somerset and Dorset border country] should be placed upon the broad gauge.'

The Great Western had dared to praise the virtues of Radstock coal, its inexhaustible abundance, its superior quality, its cheapness. Mr. Cockburn however, illustrated the contrary view by calling Mr. Paine, a Salisbury coal merchant who was selling Newcastle coal at 33s a ton and Radstock coal at 23s a ton, but who nevertheless sold two-thirds more of the former.

Then Captain George Scobell RN was examined, a director of the Wilts, Somerset & Weymouth and a partner in the Radstock coal pits, the same far-sighted gentleman who had burned his fingers with the Bath & Weymouth. He had to admit that the best test of the quality of coal was the price it would fetch. Mr. Cockburn though, was not content with such a half-hearted admission. 'For all purposes of domestic convenience this Radstock coal is an intolerable article,' he stormed, 'that, as regards pictures and furniture, it would be impossible to burn it, owing to the dust and smoke which arise from it.' He quoted a Mr. M'Culloch: 'the deepest coal-mine in England is stated to be at Radstock, near Bath; it is 409 yards from the surface, there are several small seams of coal… none exceeding 3 ft; they would scarcely be deemed worth working were it not for the scarcity of coal in that part of England'.

'Add to that, that the inconvenience of the break of gauge is nothing in the case of coal. Just consider,' he suggested, 'the difference between a load of coal and a waggonful of bullocks.'

This unexpected image was in fact quite a fair observation of the difficulties involved in carrying goods across a break of gauge. Farmers would prefer not to subject their cattle to such rough treatment, he suggested, whereas Radstock coal would positively benefit from being thrown about, because it came out of the ground in such massive lumps. The problem of tranship-ment between the gauges was inescapable, but was Radstock coal really so unpleasant? It already travelled stealthily out of its native valleys by way of the Somersetshire Coal Canal and its tramways, to Bath and the northern districts of Wiltshire and Berkshire, to satisfy an eager market. This was not proving to be the most satisfactory arrangement however, and local pit proprietors supported the assertion made by the Bath & Weymouth Railway some years before, that Radstock coal travelled by 'an ill-constructed tramroad to Midford, where the coals are unloaded and stacked, and from whence they are afterwards sent in boats by a circuitous route to Bath'. And anyway the greatest portion of coals consumed in Bath and its neighbourhood was conveyed by carts and waggons. It took two days for coal to travel fourteen miles by canal from Paulton Engine Basin to the Old Bridge at Bath. It was reckoned that a proper railway would reduce the travelling time to a couple of hours.

So the first railway to supersede these primitive transport systems was the broad gauge branch of the Wilts, Somerset & Weymouth which had been authorised in 1845. It was to run from Frome, very close in places to the long-abandoned Dorset & Somerset Canal which was used here and there to accommodate excavated soil from the railway. As a mineral line it did not bother to approach any villages along the way – Mells Road station was built twenty years later as an afterthought – but headed directly for the heart of Radstock and her pits.

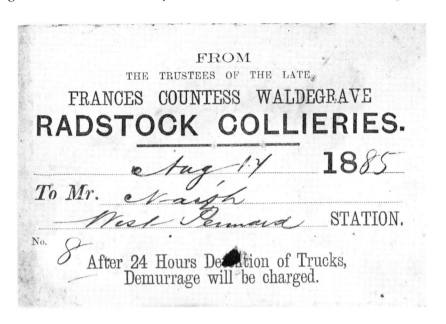

The figure whose shadow could be discerned upon the Radstock landscape at almost every turn during these times was the Right Honourable Frances Elizabeth Anne, Dowager Countess Waldegrave. She was the daughter of John Braham, a well known singer of the period, and the dimensions of her life were appropriately histrionic. She married various wealthy, noble and politically prominent men, carrying the fortune and title she acquired from the second through to the last. Her first husband had died the year she married him. Her second, the seventh Earl, she lived with in the Queen's Bench prison for six months, whither he had been sentenced for assault. From him she inherited the coal of Radstock. Her third husband she married at twenty-six. He, George Granville Harcourt, was sixty-two, and Tory MP for Oxfordshire. Her last was a liberal politician, Lord Carlingford. Her estates were large, her energy boundless and her influence all-pervading. Parcels of her land had been surveyed by the Wilts, Somerset & Weymouth Railway for their branch, and when the Great Western at last made an agreement with her to purchase, there was a large number of reciprocal clauses which granted useful rights to the Countess. She owned most of the pits in the town and the branch was calculated to terminate in the centre, adjacent to one of them, Ludlow's. She was to have a siding running directly into the colliery, and with two days' notice would be able to call upon the Great Western to take laden wagons from her junction and convey them, furnishing a 'good and efficient engine' for the purpose. Each trainload was to contain at least two hundred tons of coal and be destined no fewer than fifty miles distant, breaks of gauge notwithstanding.

The railway was opened on November 14th 1854. It was 8¾ miles long and is described wistfully some years later by the *Tourist's Guide*: 'between Frome and Radstock it traverses a very pleasant well-wooded country, much bolder as it rapidly descends the incline into the Radstock bottom, where, but for the spoil-heaps and the smoke of the collieries, the scenery would be remarkably picturesque, what with the steep hills, the narrow winding network of valleys, and the plentiful dotting of trees. Coal-dust and fumes are, however, sad enemies to romance.'

A pair of 'good and efficient engines'. The Great Western yard staff pose in front of a pannier tank and an outside-framed saddle tank at Radstock c1920.
Colin Maggs Collection

Coal-dust and fumes were, though, a necessary by-product of the valley's life-supporting industry, and for a hundred years or so the collieries and the railways worked closely together. Competition became fierce as Somerset coal started to come out at railway speed. In Bath there was a choice of Dean Forest, Ruabon, or the Wallsend coals which came by sea. So the coal of Radstock had to work hard, a local merchant taking pains to praise it thus: 'The Superiority of these coals over every other quality brought into the Bath market consists in their unusual brilliancy of heat, freedom from dust, and very great durability.' *Nota bene* Mr. Cockburn!

At a wedding celebration in Radstock a couple of years after the railway had arrived, a roomful of guests sat down to a substantial wine dinner in the Waldegrave Arms. The bridegroom was one Thomas Pilditch, an employee of the Somersetshire Coal Company, though evidently not a miner. Throughout the evening toasts were drunk, and disposed among those declamations wishing long life to Her Majesty were a pertinent selection relating to more local concerns: 'The Right Hon. the Countess Waldegrave! The Mining, Manufacturing, Agricultural and Commercial Interests of the Country! The Industrial Classes of the Community, with especial reference to the Colliers!' and, before the revels broke up at an advanced hour, the health was drunk of 'The present and prospective Railways of Somerset!'

The prospective railways of Radstock had to wait however, for some time. Too long it seems for Seward Brice, writing about the Somerset coalfield in 1867 : 'We have no doubt been rather unfortunate in respect of Railways. Several, I am afraid to say how many, attempts have been made to connect London and Bristol by means of a narrow guage [sic] line passing right through the county; but they have all failed, and at present it seems we must rest content with what the Great Western Railway will do for us. Of course any Railway will be better than none...'

The first newcomer, with better to come, was the Bristol & North Somerset which in 1873 effectively extended the branch from Frome through the town and northwards to Bristol. Carrying passengers as well as goods it immediately turned the heads of the local people from the markets of Bath, to which they had customarily travelled, towards those of Bristol. But the following year they welcomed the most dynamic arrival of all and restored their favours. This was surely the prospective railway whose health had been drunk so heartily and so unwittingly nearly twenty years before. Not only did this new line tap the Radstock coalfield and link Bath with the south coast – which would have been a pointless exercise in itself as the Wilts, Somerset & Weymouth had long since achieved the same things by a less mountainous route – but significantly it also joined, on the narrow gauge, the manufacturing Midlands and North of England with Somerset and the nascent holiday town of Bournemouth.

It was the Somerset & Dorset. And writing immediately before its triumphant single-track railway opened over the Mendips from Evercreech to Bath, D. H. Gale gives us an intimate and finely observed account of the appearance of the railway at that time.

'The stations are all of the same pattern, but differ in size in accordance with the requirements of the place. They are substantially composed of blue lias stone with Bath or Doulting stone dressings, and slate tile roofs. From the front wall of each there stands a wooden verandah, the edges of which are hung with Vandyked vallance. In nearly all the stations there are two waiting rooms and a booking office. The buildings are of English architecture, and present an attractive appearance, though they are all but one story [sic] high. The platform of each station is covered with gravel, there being at the edge two courses of blue bricks, the outer of which is rounded off. The home and distant signals in connexion with each station are worked from the station itself, the signal levers being above ground, and the machinery in a covered pit. The signals are manufactured by Saxby and Farmer. The same firm fitted the points with their patent point locking gear, which fix and keep the points secure, thus obviating the danger of running the train off or on to the wrong line, provided the signalman does his work properly...

A wonderful impression of the centre of Radstock in the early years of this century, looking east. The two railways – the Somerset & Dorset to the left and the Great Western to the right – were built in the early 1870s and came to dominate the town. The track of the valley's earlier coal transport system, the Somersetshire Coal Canal tramway, is marked by the footpath in the foreground. M. J. Tozer Collection

'At this end of the line the "packing" between the rails (which are all laid upon transoms placed across, and not longitudinally, as is the practice upon the main line of the Great Western Railway,) is of gravel. Near Radstock the cinders from the colliery engines are used for this purpose, and at other points broken stone, which being of white lias, presents a clean appearance. The whole of the work on the line has been heavy, and especially so at this end. The viaducts are numerous and are all very substantially built of white or blue lias, roughly faced, with brick turned arches. They are all very similar in design, and are handsome structures, the piers supporting the arches being graceful but strong. As the branch is only a single line the viaducts are narrower than we have been accustomed to see on broad guage [sic] double lines in this locality…

'Both the branches of railway which now pass Radstock have been constructed on the narrow gauge principle, which, as it is exclusively used on the Midland and South Western lines and as the Great Western is adopting, the plan must be considered as one of universal use. It cannot but be concluded that this rapid growth of railway accommodation whilst affording much convenience to the inhabitants will also have a highly beneficial effect upon commerce, which will be developed to a much greater extent than at present, for it must be remembered that both the road and canal communications which have until recently been the sole arteries of trade – have been in winter greatly dependant [sic] upon the weather…

'The new line, like that of the North Somerset, has a level crossing here, the gates of both crossings being only about ten yards apart. The stations are also close together. The station-house is a pretty little building. There are two platforms and a goods shed. The level crossing gates are opened and closed by levers fixed in the signal-house, which contains thirty-one switch handles. Beneath the line is a subway formed by gradients on either side. This is for the convenience of carriages going to the station…'

The new railways were at last giving consideration to the needs of local passengers. The Great Western had only been after their coal. But now the people of Radstock could travel by train too.

6

A Few Men & Many Wheelbarrows

One of the original reasons for the Great Western planning a branch to Bradford and Trowbridge was not so much the promise of coal, but the presence there of the remnants of a once great cloth manufacturing trade. The ancient woollen industry had grown up along the upper Avon valley and its tributaries, the rivers providing power for water mills to drive the fulling stocks and later the looms. They also provided good water for fulling and dyeing. It had been a cottage-based industry for two or three hundred years before the first factories arrived. These were built when steam power was introduced and new spinning and weaving equipment was developed towards the end of the eighteenth century. As the manufacturing process became more complex, factories congregated in the towns and weaving in the villages died out.

The late arrival of the railway in the Wiltshire and Somerset wool districts has often been blamed for the second place which the trade here took to that of Yorkshire. It is true that in the late 1830s the Avon valley cloth trade was depressed and the failure of the railway companies to penetrate the area adequately at that time did nothing to help. But there were many causes dating back to the beginning of the nineteenth century. Whereas, for instance, many Yorkshire mills were already steam-powered by 1800, the first steam engine in Trowbridge had yet to be installed. The Kennet & Avon Canal had not yet begun to open up the lines of industrial communication. And Frome suffered too, partly but permanently from the fact that the Dorset & Somerset Canal had failed at that vital period. In fact the opening of the Wilts, Somerset & Weymouth in 1848 marked the beginning of two or three decades of renewed prosperity for the few mills that remained, especially in Trowbridge which had become the most prominent local factory town. Over thirty steam engines were at work in the factories of Trowbridge by 1857 and the town was thriving.

The previous summer, the Wilts, Somerset & Weymouth had opened its branch through to Salisbury from the junction at Westbury. A couple of months later, towards the end of August it was made known that the Royal train would be passing down the line. Queen Victoria, Prince

Albert, the Prince of Wales and the Princesses were travelling by rail from Plymouth to Osborne House on the Isle of Wight, passing through Taunton, where the Queen looked 'somewhat unwell', and on via Bristol, Bath and Salisbury. Trowbridge responded at once to this circuitous pilgrimage, ornamented her station, decorated her factory chimneys and collected in an 'immense concourse of all classes' along the railway line. A band played and 'after a patient waiting, the expected Royal carriages rushed by like a rocket, much to the disappointment of the congregated crowds'.

Trowbridge Horticultural & Floral Exhibition in full swing beside the railway. Note that the artist has mistaken the location of the disc and crossbar signal and rooted it at the entrance to Mandry's refreshment tent!   Wiltshire Libraries

Agriculture benefited too by the railway. That year the 7th Annual Trowbridge Floral and Horticultural Show was held in a spacious field near the railway, though unfortunately the weather seems to have been wet. The Frome Cheese Show, which was first organised some years later and is still held today, also dates from this first flush of enthusiasm for the railway.

By the 1890s, Trowbridge had established itself as the county's administrative centre. But, though communications had been opened up and Somerset coal could be obtained more cheaply and finished goods carried to markets more speedily, by the turn of the century Trowbridge had only six working mills left. Bradford-on-Avon had only one, Chippenham one and Melksham none. Frome, which still had some working mills, was described by the *Tourist's Guide* as 'an

GREAT WESTERN RAILWAY.

Frome Cheese, Butter, Horse, Cattle, &c., Show.

Riding and Driving by Ladies.
PRIZES £600.

On WEDNESDAY, September 25th,

EXCURSION TICKETS WILL BE ISSUED TO

FROME

FROM	Time of Starting.		Return Fares, Third Class.	Time of Return.
	A.M.	A.M.		P.M. P.M.
SWINDON	5 45	7 35	3/-	5.45 or 7.45
CHIPPENHAM ...	6 18	10 10	2/6	3.24, 5.45,
MELKSHAM	6 33	10 27	2/-	or 7.45.
SALISBURY	7 45	9 15	3/3	
WILTON..	7 53	9 23	3/-	
WISHFORD	7 59	9 29		7.9 or 8.55
WYLYE	8 9	9 39	2/6	
CODFORD	8 17	9 48	2/2	
HEYTESBURY	8 25	9 55	1/9	
WARMINSTER	8 35	10 7	1/3	7.9,5.30,8.55
CRANMORE	—	9 42	1/3	6.5, 6.39,
SHEPTON MALLET ...	—	9 29	1/6	or 9.29.
WELLS...	—	9 15	2/-	‡ Special through train.

A Special Train will leave Frome at 5.30 p.m. for Westbury.

Children under Twelve, Half-price. No Luggage Allowed.

The Tickets are not transferable. Should an Excursion or Cheap Ticket be used for any other Station than those named upon it, or by any other Train than those specified, it will be rendered void, and therefore the fare paid will be liable to forfeiture, and the full Ordinary Fare will become chargeable.

For information respecting Tourist and Pleasure Party arrangements, and Excursion and Special Trips on the Great Western Railway, application should be made to Mr. C. Kislingbury, Divisional Superintendent, Temple Meads Station, Bristol; or at any of the Stations.

Paddington, Sept., 1907. JAMES C. INGLIS, General Manager.

(Bristol, 3,500 R. 8vo, 2 sides.) Arrowsmith, Printer, Quay Street, Bristol. (B 813)

old town and a hideous. With two or three worthy exceptions the streets are narrow, crooked, steep, and irregularly built, not to say dilapidated'. Westbury, it said, was 'no more interesting and attractive than Frome'.

An old town and a hideous – the rooftops of Frome. 'While other parts of the country have suffered through industrial strife, our labouring population have not been lured to their ruin...' – Somerset Standard, *Christmas 1897.*

The last country mill factory was in the village of Farleigh Hungerford, once planned to be served by the main line of the Bath & Weymouth Railway. It worked until 1910 and was derelict by the time Edward Thomas passed that way upon his bicycle in 1913, in pursuit of spring. Just previously he had stopped in Bradford-on-Avon to the sound of 'jackdaws flying and crying' over the town.

'I dismounted by the empty "Lamb" inn, with a statue of a black-faced lamb over its porch, and sat on the bridge. The Avon ran swift, but calm and dull, down under the bridge and away westward. The town hill rises from off the water, covered as with scales with stone houses of countless varieties of blackened gray and many gables, and so steep that the roofs of one horizontal street are only just higher than the doorsteps of the one above. A brewery towers from the mass at the far side, and, near the top, a factory with the words "For Sale" printed on its roof in huge letters. And the smoke of factories blew across the town. The hilltop above the houses is crested with beeches and rooks' nests against the blue. The narrow space between the foot of the hill and the river is occupied by private gardens, a church and its churchyard yews and chestnuts, and by a tall empty factory based on the river bank itself, with a notice "To Let".' Bradford's last mill had been long decaying.

Bradford-on-Avon photographed in the early 1870s, no longer a flourishing wool town. The railway crosses the river on its original timber trussed bridge under the protection of a spindly disc and crossbar signal. The bridge was subsequently rebuilt in steel. Wiltshire Libraries

It certainly seemed as if the railway always left things too late. In 1874 a station was provided at Holt, which had been the junction for the Devizes branch since 1857. Once, Melksham was going to be the place favoured for this privilege and Brunel had offered to move his wool towns' branch over a bit to accommodate the connection with the local company. But the meeting place was changed to give easier access for Devizes traffic onto the Limpley Stoke valley line to Bath, and so perhaps Holt should not have been ungrateful.

The local demand for rail facilities can hardly be said to have received a responsive hearing however. This new station provided the first opportunity since the opening day revels seventeen years before, for villagers to join trains on their own doorstep. Proper road access had to wait another three years, goods traffic facilities another year, ladies' toilets another seventeen years, a canopy over the platform yet another seventeen years. At first travellers had even had to climb over the rails to reach the island platform, until a footbridge was built.

The largest industry here was Beaven's leatherworks. The factory required, among other things, the rather unpleasant raw materials of skins and dog manure which were brought by rail. To compensate for this the owners provided a generous annual works outing. Nearby on the Avon at Staverton, was an isolated country cloth mill of grand proportions, in which the district's earliest power looms had been installed in the late 1830s. And though the Wilts, Somerset

& Weymouth's first section of railway was laid down along the Avon valley as far as this point and crossed the river very close to the mill, there seems to have been no use made by the one of the other until after the mill had been converted into a milk condensery by Nestlé's in 1897.

A passenger halt was opened here some eight years later followed by a loading bay at Holt in 1909. Private sidings at Staverton were not built until 1934, a belated reponse to the dairy industry which the railway itself had stimulated as much in this area as it had down in Somerset.

A mixed goods train waits in the up platform at Holt Junction while the employees of Beavan's leatherworks, in their Sunday best, anticipate a day's outing to Portsmouth in the summer of 1905. The awning has not arrived yet.

Some areas changed their characters more completely than others. The railway came too late to resuscitate the cloth trade at Westbury, but in 1856 iron ore was quarried here for the first time, by George Greenwell, who also managed Lady Waldegrave's Radstock collieries. Great, towering smelting furnaces were built beside Westbury railway station, like a set for Lang's "Metropolis"; a demonic companion for that huge horse carved into the chalk escarpment beyond the town. Today the white pennant of a cement works chimney, beside the London main line, provides a strangely more tolerable contrast, but Westbury is only a shadow of its former self. Some of the wool towns further west had turned to more closely related specialised manufacturing as trade declined and consolidated. At Castle Cary for example, enterprising men had introduced twine making and horse-hair weaving early in the nineteenth century. At Bruton it was silk. But their factories never intruded or changed their essentially country town characters.

Nevertheless, during the period up to the First World War, before motorised transport became widespread, the railway was part of everyday life such as it had never been before and has not been since. Some towns were lucky with their rail connection, pawns at the mercy of the railway companies' fundamental obligation to generate a financial return for their investors. Had the Great Western not sought to block the South Western's advance to the West, Bruton, for example, might have remained rail-less as it had been in the Bath & Weymouth's plan. Had the Great Western not sought to use the Weymouth line for part of its own advance to the West, Bruton would have remained on a mere branch. Some towns achieved a good railway by corporate effort. Others had a fast London main line thrust upon them.

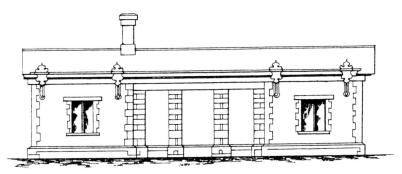

An elevation of the down platform building at Bruton station 'designed and executed by' Brunel and R. J. Ward, from a book of drawings compiled in 1870 by J. W. Grover. Adrian Vaughan, however, states R. P. Brereton to be author of this exquisite little structure. 'The building is of Gothic character with walls of fitted rubble and Ashlar masonry, and with a slate roof etc, and a cantilever roof the whole length of the building 10 feet wide.' It cost £1031. The left hand part was a waiting room. The right contained urinals. The middle section was a recessed shelter, behind which were store rooms. The main building on the up platform was stylistically identical. Witham, Castle Cary, Sparkford and other stations down the Wilts, Somerset & Weymouth line had similar buildings. Today Bruton station looks like a bus stop.   John Froud Collection

The people of Bruton had recognised their good fortune when the Wilts, Somerset & Weymouth opened through the town, and turned out for a festive welcome. On Monday September 1st 1856 the first down train from Frome contained Thomas Graham the Superintendent, and R. J. Ward the Engineer admiring his handiwork. Perhaps the locals were taken by surprise for then they organised a celebration. On Wednesday the sun shone, the arches which spanned the line were decorated with evergreens and banners. The bells of St Mary's church were rung out across the town, and a procession wound through the streets to an open-air dinner near the railway. There were the Blue Boys, the men and women of the hospital preceded by the oldest member in a Bath chair (he had been born in 1760), the Blue Ball Friendly Society from the local inn, the factory workers, the Milborne Port Band, the Band of Hope, a body of otherwise unaffiliated men and women with tickets, children of the parochial schools and householders of the town. The exclamations they carried on their banners read 'Prosperity to the Bruton Railway' and, as if to justify their astonishment, 'Long Expected, Come at Last'. They all sat down to beef, beer and buns, and shortly afterwards there began the Old English

Bruton station staff and a permanent way gang pose for the camera c1905. The shallow stone-arch bridge was later demolished.
Colin Maggs Collection

Sports. 'The different trains as they passed close to the scene of enjoyment were vehemently cheered by the vast crowd and were as heartily cheered in return by the passengers.'

That same year, beyond the wit of those engaged in Old English Sports, the broad gauge Somerset Central Railway from Highbridge to Glastonbury was planning its eastward extension to join with the Wilts, Somerset & Weymouth line. Its ambition as a local branch railway was, in Mr. Cockburn's words, to afford *real* accommodation to the district and to achieve substance as a through route. Frome had been a favourite objective, but the easier line to Bruton was the one authorised by Parliament. The connection was to have been some little way west of Bruton station, beyond Cole village, where the railway crosses the Brue. It was a connection that somehow signifies the antipathy between the Great Western and the S&D, a connection, almost completed, not only of two lengths of track, but in the event, of two railway empires. The earthworks were formed but it appears the track was never laid. In fact the Somerset Central bridged over the Weymouth line in order to link with the Dorset Central heading north from Blandford, and from that time on, those two companies, which amalgamated as the Somerset & Dorset in 1862, were part of the narrow gauge system. The junction that never was, could have made of Bruton an important changing place, but the S&D station at Cole is no more, the embankments trackless, and the prosperity wished on the Bruton Railway has served it well.

Coincidentally with the opening of the Somerset & Dorset main line, as Gale observed, the Wilts, Somerset & Weymouth was converted from broad gauge to narrow, and, if it achieved nothing else in its eventful life, the Somerset & Dorset could be said thus to have forced a major victory for the narrow gauge. Pragmatism had prevailed over genius. The Radstock coal owners had insisted on it. During the next twenty years nearly all these narrow gauge, single-track railways were gradually doubled to ease the flow of traffic and allow greater competition. The ascendancy of what now became the standard gauge railway was assured for the duration of the British Empire, and the Great Western's long-held desire to reach the West Country by a direct route must have seemed attainable.

To realise the dream, a new railway from Stert to Westbury and another from Castle Cary to Langport would have to be built. Railway construction technology had now achieved the assurance of fifty years' rapid development, but politics and finance could be as obstructive as ever. In 1882 the Berks & Hants Extension Railway which owned the line from Hungerford to Devizes, was amalgamated with the Great Western, so the following year both the Stert to Westbury and the Langport parts were attempted. But it was 1900 before Westbury station was enlarged and became a double junction.

In May 1903 the *Castle Cary Visitor* reported on the 'Langport Railway': 'After years of waiting and many promises, the Directors have done something towards giving the new line a start. The contract of the work has been given to Mr. C. J. Wills of Manchester, and while we write a few men and many wheelbarrows may be seen at the Cary end of the line.' And in the

Many men and no wheelbarrows prepare the earthworks for the embryonic Somerton viaduct 1905.

summer of 1906 this assemblage completed its labours. The stretch of the Wilts, Somerset & Weymouth between here and Westbury became part of that Great Way West as planned in earlier and more visionary days. Instead of travelling through the Vale of the White Horse and around by way of Bristol to reach Devon, passengers from Paddington could now speed on long gentle stretches of line, arcing through the Vale of Pewsey and down via Taunton: ample competition for the old wiggling rival South Western line through Salisbury and Yeovil. West of Castle Cary the new line pursued the River Cary across the Cary moor, through Keinton Mandeville and Charlton Mackrell where spacious modern stations were provided, passing by a long high embankment and five elegant arches of brick over the Cary just outside Somerton, and on from King Arthur's Country in to King Alfred's.

As we have seen, the importance of all these railways to the local economies and communities was always, and would remain, of secondary consideration. The length of railway running across Farmer Brown's fields, lately a single line of broad gauge 'baulk road', was now a fine standard gauge double-track line. And even as the Cornish Riviera Express hurtled through Bruton and Castle Cary, raising them to main line status, the comfortable-looking station buildings maintained an unpretentious air which seemed self-consciously to declare that really they belonged to the local Weymouth line. Which they did, for the expresses never stopped. Capital investment was only made available, even in those days, for the long distance routes or to exploit a lucrative source of supply or demand: a valuable raw material like coal or a particular manufactured product. In the 1930s short-cut deviations were built to by-pass the stations at Frome and Westbury. Speed and fuel efficiency were paramount.

C. L. Caddy

PART 3

A Frome train glides into Radstock Great Western station behind a '517' tank. The elevated signalbox must have given extensive views of the line, but it was shortly to be replaced by the more familiar squat building, c1905.　　　　M. J. Tozer Collection
Overleaf is the same view more than fifty years later. Ex GWR 2-6-2 tank No 4567 brings a Frome train over the Great Western level crossing into Radstock station. Evidently a Bristol train is also expected. The date is April 8th 1958. Passenger trains were withdrawn 18 months later.
　　　　R.E. Toop

7
PRETTY ONCE

It must have been 1963. The old North Somerset station building at Radstock was being pulled down and replaced by an arc of glowing plate-glass shops, and where the platform had once been were their smooth pale terracotta backs. The other half of the station remained over the tracks, unbalanced, like a man with one arm. The old, wooden up-starting signal had become obscured by the new block, and a steel replacement had been put up, oddly, in the middle of the left-over platform. The signal box still squatted here, commanding the level crossing. Beside the gates stood a long-necked water column, awkwardly cramped by the new shopping parade. At the far end was the Post Office, staring across the square at the seriously Victorian Hall and Institute.

Turning left outside the Post Office, the footway led into a long echoing passage which disgorged it at the foot of Frome Hill. Above the passage lay a span of railway tracks. Once, these rails from Frome had terminated short of here when coal was the only quest, and Frome Hill had run as a straight highway into the town. However the broad gauge mineral branch of the Wilts, Somerset & Weymouth, running through the pretty vales below Mells Down, had been linked up eventually to the North Somerset line from Bristol, crossing Frome Hill with a clearance of only six or seven feet to reach it. For this reason the road had been diverted and the old way made into a subterranean tunnel for the pedestrian.

Up Frome Hill out of the town past the grey white-stone colliery workshop buildings, the intriguing gloom of Ludlow's Pit could be glimpsed beyond the gates and conifers. The square chimney, part stone, part brick, braced with rusting steel, rose above the embedded railway tracks. The rails, sometimes undiscernible in the cinders, crossed the road in uneven ruts, and just beyond was a crumbling stone shed with large timber doors. Opaque windows, cobwebbed within and grimewashed without, concealed a mysterious vehicle bearing the name *Mercury*. In front of it was a huge wooden buffer with which to wheedle wagons about the yard. This strange tractor lay silent and contemplative in its garage. No pit-head wheels spun, no steam hissed, no sooty breeze blew down. Beneath the chimney lay the great black Lancashire boilers, russet rivetted, rusted, quiet and cold. Bindweed bound the safety valves. Grass was growing where colliers' boots would once have scuffed the dust.

Over Frome Hill the wide, open yard was black with ground coal and empty. Groundblack and evergreen were the hues of the coalscape. Up on the hill were the batches of Tyning.

Wispy grasses pushed palely through the waste. Rows of ashen cottages arranged themselves in terraces on the slopes, neatly gabled at each end. Pinnacles and pediments of the dissenting chapels pointed, together with the clock tower on the market roof, in the direction of heaven. For many a man this trodden earth and the workings that lay beneath it begged the questions asked of him by the circuit preachers, concerning heaven's comfort and the fires of hell.

A busy spring-like afternoon in the centre of Radstock c1905. The Great Western crossing gates are firmly closed in favour of the pedestrian and the horse-drawn carriages.

Unable to resist the lure of the town, the road descended gently back round the diverting elbow of Frome Hill towards the twin level crossings, the twin signal boxes and the twin stations. The Great Western and the Somerset & Dorset occupied half the town between them. At the centre they ran parallel, only yards apart. Northbound trains on the former headed west. Northbound trains on the latter headed east. Winding between them in a shallow cleft flowed the brook, and arching low over the water was the stone bridge. Beside the brook came Frome Hill, now on the level, meeting the A367 Bath road at right angles. It was this turnpike road which, diverted off the hill tops from the line of the Roman Fosse Way, dropped down into the valley to cross the tracks and span the brook. Thus, squeezed into the space between the level crossings was the soul of the town; the conjunction of highways, a helpful black and white signpost, a telephone box, a couple of shops, a tiny newsagent's lock-up cantilevered over the river bank, the bridge, a fine row of elms and much more that did not reveal itself to the casual glance.

In the face of the traveller leaving the town centre, the delicate white gates of the Great Western first barred the carriageway. There would be no option but to wait until the black, work-worn pannier tank had panted and creaked its rumbling wagons over the crossing. An enormous wheel turned rapidly up in the signalbox and the ghostly gates moved slowly and silently across the road to close against the trains.

In something of a hurry by now, the traveller crossed the tracks and the bridge, approaching the marginally less ethereal, but no less firmly closed gates of the Somerset & Dorset. Away up into the Mendips climbed the steel lines, curving, canting, stretching to a vanishing point beyond the trees. A melancholy expectancy seemed to drift down into the valley. This was the betrayed line, the passionate line. It had been won by struggle and would struggle again in defeat. The railway had been possessed of strong principles and a wilful determination. To the end it only grudgingly accepted the rationales of diesel power, 'college-boy' management and even nationalisation. It would fight to the end rather than surrender, but it would still have the last laugh, continuing to run steam trains for three months after the Western Region had triumphantly declared itself rid of that outmoded vapour.

The soul of Radstock: the Great Western level crossing and, beyond, the S&D crossing. The subway under the S&D can be seen to the left of the very distinguished looking lamppost.

M. J. Tozer Collection

They were both Western region now, these twin stations, placed side by side and serving the small town of maybe six thousand people. They gave the town two faces. One bore the character of the Somerset & Dorset, and the other, that of the Great Western. So at once it was slow and dirty, smoky and grim, exploited and abhorred, chapel, charity and cabbage patches, and again it was patrician, county provincial, clean and prim, C. of E. and mown lawns. It was a town of Two Railways. The traditions of the one held a stranglehold on the hopes of the other. In the end they took them both away.

A Bath train rolls down over the S&D crossing behind a Standard class 4 2-6-0 on a damp May afternoon in 1963.

A hoot far off and a whispering gave way to the onslaught of a local train of three green coaches which, having descended the bank behind the hunched bulk of a Standard Class 4 locomotive, rolled its great weight across the road and jarred to rest in the station.

Had the traveller been captivated entirely by contemplation of the gates, the alternative route – the slipway under the tracks of the Somerset & Dorset – would have remained unseen beside the road. It was often flooded, yet down here in the dark beneath the railway had been another level crossing. Once the Somersetshire Coal Canal tramway had lowered itself gradually down to this depth behind the down platform of the S&D station. It had crossed the sliproad, burrowed firstly under the highway and then the railway, curving away then towards the tiny gasworks, Old Pit and Clandown. Down at this level too, in the early years of the last century, water had filled the terminal basin of the Somersetshire Coal Canal itself. The valley floor held a host of secrets from the past.

Above, supported on black girders, was the North 'B' signalbox of cream-painted timber. Beyond the darkness and the eternal pools of water, the slipway turned sharply to the right and rose up to the station. A flight of steep stone steps climbed by a shorter route up into the market place. A cluster of lamps and notice boards were gathered at the top of the steps. Ahead stood the Bell Hotel, gabled and bay-windowed, the market building, glazed and a little fragile, and the more ancient Waldegrave Arms, solid, tall, grey and unadorned. Between these buildings the roads left the market place: the Old Road which climbed steeply out of the valley and forked into the Bath and Bristol roads, the hundred and fifty year old Turnpike which short-cut them both on a gentler gradient, and a pair of lanes which wandered off to lesser destinations.

Market Day. A Photograph taken from the S&D signalbox around 1906.

A shriek of steam from the far end of the station, and billows of soft smoke celebrated the departure of the Bath local. It would follow the route that the horses had taken on the tramway years before, and the coal boats on the narrow canal before that. One replaced the other, the valley gave and took.

An undated view (probably the early 1930s) across the Radstock valley showing the head gear and surface buildings of Middle Pit. Just behind are the old cinema and the gasworks. The colliery closed in 1933 but the chimney remained as a monument to the coal industry in the town. Demolition began in March 1987.

Just past the Waldegrave Arms (the Lord of the Manor gave and took too), in Combe End, was the old picture house, once called the Palace; a severe, large gabled and unpalatial frontage which seemed to be waiting, optimistically even, for the local youngsters to crowd again through its doorways. In a previous incarnation it had been one of Radstock's fine collection of Methodist chapels. Behind it, the enormously tall tapering chimney of Middle Pit spired, as if the mine were trying to reach as far into the sky as it did into the earth. A narrow cindertrack turned off the road between the high, dark walls of the picture house and the pit, and here was the entrance into an enchanted and forgotten hinterland.

Behind the façades and the faces of the town lay a grass-grown and unfrequented wilderness. Here the Clandown brook joined the Radstock brook. Here the Clandown tramway once used to bring coal-laden wagons down to the canal basin, and in later years used to link up with the Coal Canal tramway which replaced the canal. Here was Middle Pit, strewn about with corroded, oozing batteries. Here was the small green gas-holder, empty of gas, its pit filled with thick brown water and decaying leaves. Up the valley a short distance was the site of Old Pit, the first to have been sunk in the town, now barely discernible. Here were tracks in the undergrowth, rust-flaking spikes loose in rotten, fibrous sleepers and brambles low overhead. These sidings which had replaced the tramway were, in turn, being reclaimed by the organic processes of nature. Here was a black Tyer's ground frame on a small timber platform. Its levers leant into

Clandown colliery branch junction photographed on May 25th 1963. Radstock North B signalbox and the S&D crossing can be seen in the distance, the main line climbing up to the right. This connection was probably made around 1886 when the main line was doubled, the coal traffic having previously used the old tramway route, under the main line, up behind the station and into the goods yard. The branch had been converted from tramway to standard gauge and opened up the valley to Clandown in September 1882. Clandown Colliery was situated on top of the hill and was reached by a steep rope-worked incline. The pit closed in 1929 and thereafter the branch got shorter as Middle Pit followed it in 1933, and, finally, the gasworks siding closed in 1955. The junction was removed in 1961 but the overgrown track remained for some years.

the bushy overgrowth. Here was a notice board on a post, tawny paint faded and weathered: 'All engines, other than those of the 0-4-0 type, are prohibited from passing beyond this board. By Order'. The branch had been severed from the main line and a length of crooked iron fencing fell across the rails. A greying signal post poked the sky with its tiny red finial. Two crimson and white signal arms lay at the foot, smashed, where they had been dropped unneeded, unheeded. This backwater branch had made do with one signal, an arm for each direction and no lamps or coloured glasses, for it was not used after dark. The Dazzlers, and later the Sentinels and Pugs, the small, quaintly nicknamed locomotives addressed by the notice board's qualifying phrase, used to squeal laboriously around this curve collecting wagons of coal from the pits, delivering them to the gas works or bringing empty ones to the sidings. The formation of the old tramway could be seen at a lower level in a large swampy triangular fringe of long grass. It came into this clearing under the black iron girders of the railway bridge from the direction of the station. It left beneath another, heading the opposite way towards the collieries at Welton. Butted close up against the brick embankment of the main line was a row of cottages, down at the original ground level, their roofs now as high as the rails. Once, their long front gardens had swept down to the brook.

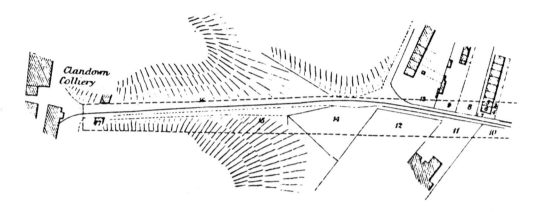

PARISH OF MIDSOMER NORTON

Above – Part of the Parliamentary plan showing the incline up to the Clandown Colliery, 1873.

Below – a view of Clandown c1905. At the top is the colliery with waste batches at either side. Descending to the right is the rope-worked railway incline, popularly known as the "gug" – a term meaning the miners' road. Nearly twenty years after the colliery closed Messrs Wheeler & Co were established on the site manufacturing brieze blocks. In the 1960s Radstock coal was being mined for use at Portishead power station. The ash was returned to Clandown where it became the raw material for the brieze blocks.

Opposite – A view of the pithead at about the same period.   Dennis Rendell Collection

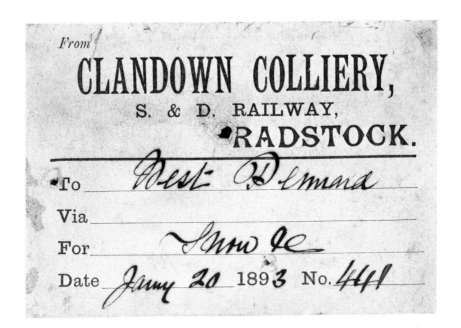

John Smith
Collection

Above – Stanier 8F 2-8-0 No 48468 leaving Radstock in a cloud of steam. May 4th 1963.

Opposite – The brick-arched bridge which carried the S&D over the Welton line of the Somersetshire Coal Canal tramway. This fell out of use in the 1880s when Old Welton and Welton Hill Collieries were connected to the GWR.

Nothing remained of the tramway now either. Stone sleeper blocks and plate rails perhaps were buried somewhere beneath these banks of earth. The "Marble Arch" had been demolished by this time – the low tunnel beyond the station yard which had carried a steep rail incline out of the town, over the tramway and the S&D main line, up to the Waldegrave waste tips at Tyning. It had been a well-known feature in the town; so lengthy because of the sharp skew angle at which the lines crossed, so low because it was only made for horses to pass through, and yet it lasted for so long – over a hundred years – and the railway company even built, bought or borrowed special dwarf locomotives to fit inside it – the Dazzlers, Sentinels and Pugs.

As the curious explorer returned to the cinder track, trying to piece together the fragments of the past that were so clearly visible tucked into corners of the town, the picture house and Middle Pit rose darkly at either side, the powerless batteries, kicked into the grass, spoke of decaying industry. A reclamation company had occupied the pit premises since the mid-fifties, and men worked here now refining zinc and aluminium into ingots, and recovering copper and lead from scrap. There was a cold air here, breathing a hint of the horrors which must have embraced many unfortunate souls labouring beneath this soil. The breathless explorer hurried along the track to the sunlight and safety of the market place and, as suspected, the crossing gates were once again pulled across the road. A parcels train in the S&D station, clouded in steam, was waiting to tackle the climb into the hills.

Driver Emery carefully fills the tank of S&DJR 0-4-0 No 45A – one of the Radstock 'Dazzlers' – outside the locomotive shed, where they were photographed by H.C. Casserley in March 1929. To paraphrase Chris Handley who provided this print, you can almost smell that unique combination of oil and steam that pervaded such romantically gloomy corners of the railway system.

'Radstock was pretty once,' says the *Tourist's Guide*, 'very pretty, – but black spoil heaps and smoke-belching engine-chimneys sadly detract from its natural beauties.'

Challenged to consider what season best suited the character of this town and landscape, the mind's eye pictured firstly the melancholy and wistful moods of late autumn. Rooks rasping high in the leafless, lifeless elms, and distant voices sounding clearly across the valley, shortly to be dulled by falling mist and grey rain, all seemed to echo the spirit of Mendip. Would spring ever really come to those bleak hills that formed the central rampart of the range, as it did to its dells and combes?

And then came a recollection of the bite of crisp air and the long shadows of a low wintry-red sun reflecting in the snow and steam as the local train worked hard out on the road to Wellow. It had been a bitter winter that year. Snow had drifted and imprisoned whole trains on the highest parts of the line. Now this had melted away into the rich Somerset soil as the rebirth of the year began. Three more summers would see the Somerset & Dorset to its grave, and the spark that fired the lives of many men would die with it.

Already the long, heavy holiday expresses which used to echo on the banks, struggling up through the hills, no longer came this way, revealing the extent to which the line had been deprived of its usefulness. Coal too, the mineral that fashioned the people and the landscape, was becoming uneconomic to win with an inevitability that no reassurances could stem. Three thousand tons a day were still being brought to the surface and much of it despatched by rail, but despite the desperate last-minute modernising touches made to them in their dying years, these collieries would all too soon be swept away.

There were just two Radstock pits left working the North Somerset coalfield now. Writhlington lay secluded in the wooded valley of the Radstock brook, east of the town, served by the old Somerset & Dorset. Kilmersdon stood spread out on Haydon Hill to the south, connected to the old Great Western. The workings of both were deep and difficult and only in recent years joined underground. Both pits still wound coal to the surface by steam power though electric plant was planned. Kilmersdon was usually referred to locally as Haydon and the atmosphere held a little of the great clamour that once must have rung across the town. Overalled miners with broad North Somerset talk gave life to the landscape; around three hundred men worked here now. Steam arose from apertures. A locomotive wobbled and banged wagons as large as itself in twos or threes. Dumpy grey lorries bounced across the yard stirring clouds of black dust into the otherwise clear air. Clangs echoed from the pit-head as the cage prepared to descend into the earth. A train of wagons was brought across the public road. If you spoke pleasantly to the driver there was always the possibility of being asked up onto the dark hot footplate as the locomotive heaved itself into motion. It accelerated with brisk huffs of dirty brown smoke which spread itself around the old women talking on the pavement. Away along the uneven track, closely bordered by blackberry and hawthorn, the train lurched and banged from side to side, on towards the head of the rope incline. From the hillside beyond, its arrival could be detected by the steam blowing off into the haze among the trees.

As the Great Western line lay in the valley below the pit, the coal, having been brought up from perhaps fifteen hundred feet under the surface of the hilltop, had to endure a descent down the outside of that same hill in order to reach the railway. This was contrived with the assistance of a large drum mounted on a horizontal axis and sheltered inside a crumbling stone-built shed. The rambling railway from the pit-head approached the shed and forked, passing either side of it and, immediately beyond it, plunged at a considerable angle to the floor of the valley below. Before reaching the bottom, the two lines converged again and finally connected by tight curves in a triangular junction with a siding on the Frome branch.

When a train of wagons full of coal was gathered at the top and a train of empties beneath, the operation began. A loaded wagon was attached to one end of a steel rope, which passed back through a rectangular opening in the front wall of the squat shed onto the winding drum. The

Steam blowing off among the trees ... The head of the incline at Kilmersdon.

rope re-emerged from the building and descended the incline on runners to be hooked onto an empty wagon below. Between the tracks at the crest were two long white steel levers, upon which, on account of their length and the shallow angle of their projection, a fair downward force could be exerted by the weight of one man. This apparatus was positioned so that its operator could stand commanding the descent of one vehicle and the simultaneous ascent of another before him. The loaded wagon was shunted to the edge of the precipice as the pressure upon one of the levers released a brake bearing on the massive drum groaning in the shed.

An empty wagon is brought to the top of the incline. The Peckett waits to collect. Both photographs by Philip Fowler.

Continued release of the brake allowed the huge weight of the wagon to roll slowly, stealthily and with unaccustomed grace down between the tall hedges and the frequent telegraph poles towards its ascending partner. The two passed and drew apart again, one apparently diminishing in size as it sank to the foot, the other looming upwards and jumping with a hollow clang as it arrived on the level ground. In this way the string of loaded coal wagons at the summit transformed into a string of empty ones, and ultimately these left for the pit-head behind the Peckett locomotive. Thus Kilmersdon despatched her coal.

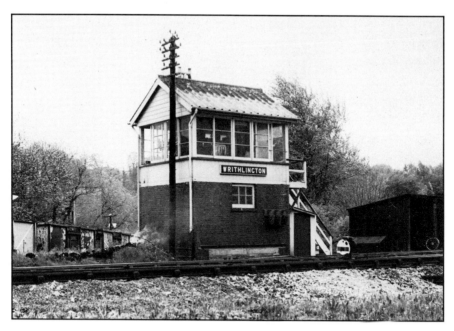

Writhlington signalbox photographed on May 18th 1963. Behind the box is the colliery, almost entirely hidden in the trees.
C. L. Caddy

FROM THE
WRITHLINGTON COLLIERIES, RADSTOCK.

No. 20   Dec 19   190

Mrs. J Baker &

Redcliff Wh.   Station.

SIMPSON'S PATENT

8

7 - 5 - 5

'A mile from Radstock,' wrote Gale in 1874, 'is the Home-farm viaduct of seven arches being one for the road and six for the farming purposes. In the bottom of the valley and close by the stream is the Writhlington pit, and a couple of hundred feet high on the opposite side of the hill is Braysdown colliery, which is connected with the line by a steep gradient down which the trucks are let by wire ropes.'

It was mid-morning, March 6th, ninety-two years later. The last passenger train to work off the S&D could have been observed approaching the coal tips of Radstock rather slowly. The creaking brakes laboured the coaches entirely to a halt just past Writhlington colliery. Heads peered out of windows. Unkind suggestions were made for the delay.

At 7.30 that morning, all the points and signals at Writhlington signalbox had been disconnected. A pilotman and a handsignalman had been on duty since seven. Now the crossover points were being clamped by hand and the train was about to reverse onto the up line. This operation held up the last rites for about twenty minutes and wise participants, observing that disaster had not befallen them, declared the party to be working wrong line. So, with 48706 and 80043 easing into their pace again, the train restarted. The reason for running single line between Writhlington and Midsomer Norton became clear as soon as the train had passed through Radstock and opened up for the bank: that sneaky connection, that dying embrace, another junction hitherto unbuilt between the S&D and the Great Western. The down line track had been slewed over to join up with the old arch-rival in the early hours, to provide a link that history and railway politics had denied the local economy for so long. So passed the first train of that sad, bitter Sunday and the rest of the day was as leisurely for the men in Writhlington box as the dawn had been eventful. What memories it must have stirred!

Lower Writhlington colliery, one of the most easterly in the Radstock coalfield, had been opened in 1829. It lay snuggled down in the valley of the Wellow brook very near to the Somersetshire Coal Canal tramway to which it was connected by a short branch. Braysdown colliery was another of the Writhlington group initially. Situated up on the hill immediately to the north, it started winding coal in the 1840s, but aloofly ignored the inarticulate transport system in the valley below. The SCC tramway carted coal from Writhlington eastwards to Midford, to the Kennet & Avon and Wilts & Berks Canals which served much of Wiltshire and Berkshire as well as Bath and Bristol. This arrangement held until the Great Western arrived in

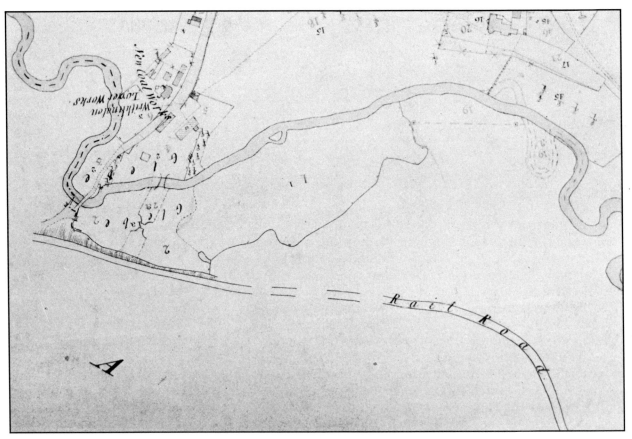

A plan of Writhlington parish drawn in 1830, showing the new colliery and the Rail Road – the Somersetshire Coal Canal
tramway.   S.R.O.
Opposite – Bransdown pithead some nine years after it had closed down.

the centre of Radstock in 1854 presenting, as we have seen, a very attractive opportunity for all the collieries within reach of the transhipment sidings. The following year Braysdown was connected to the SCC tramway by a steep, rope-worked incline, more or less opposite the Writhlington branch. At this period both collieries started to use the tramway in a westerly direction to reach the Great Western at Radstock.

The coal masters at Writhlington colliery were always averse to the high charges of the tramway and the tolls charged by the ubiquitous Lady Waldegrave for coal travelling onto the Great Western. To avoid all of these and the Waldegrave estates, a meandering tramway worked by horses and ropes was constructed around 1867 over the hill to the south of the pit and down into the next valley for direct transhipment to the Great Western. On top of the hill was a roadside coal depot, noticed by Edward Thomas on his westward pilgrimage.

'From this high land … midway between the valleys of the Frome on the left and the Midford brook on the right – we looked far on either side over valleys of mist. The hollow land on the right, which contained Radstock coalfield, many elm trees, and old overgrown mounds of coal refuse, was vague, and drowsed in the summer-like mist: the white smoke of the collieries drifted slowly in horizontal bands athwart the mist. The voices of lambs rose up, the songs of larks descended, out of the mist. Rooks cawed from field to field. Carts met us or passed us coming from Road, Freshford, Frome, and other places, to load up coal from the store by the side of the road, which is joined to the distant colliery by a miniature railway, steep and straight.'

Head gears gaunt on grass-grown pit banks, seams abandoned years ago;
Drop a stone and listen for its splash in flooded dark below…
– W. H. Auden

When the S&D was built in 1874 following the course of the SCC tramway between Radstock and Midford, Braysdown swapped its link with the tramway and the Great Western, for exchange sidings on the north side of the S&D main line. The track of the old tramway, however, still ran more or less beside the main line from Writhlington into Radstock, and it was not until 1886 that its course was straightened out and converted into a standard gauge siding, retaining a sharp curving loop into Writhlington colliery. This provided at last an outlet for Writhlington coal onto the S&D, in addition to the hill-top tramway which still ran over to the

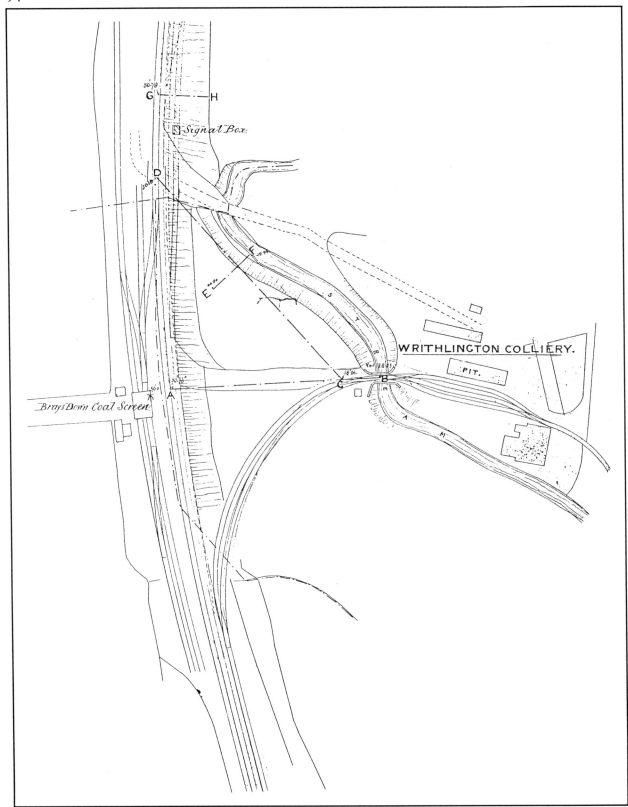

G   H

Signal Box.

D

L

E

WRITHLINGTON COLLIERY.

PIT.

C   B

Brays Down Coal Screen

A

Great Western. The latter had fallen out of use by 1940 but the former remained until the colliery itself closed down.

A block post was established at Writhlington soon after the S&D main line first opened. Perhaps because Writhlington coal did not at first travel on the S&D, and because Braysdown was up on the hill out of sight, this signalbox was named after the next nearest village – about ¾ mile away – Foxcote (Foxcote colliery did not send coal by the S&D either!). The cabin was opened in May 1875 and was sited on the south side of the line just to the east of the bridge over the Peasedown to Writhlington road. It is remembered chiefly for its part in and proximity to the horrific Foxcote accident of 1876 in which thirteen people died. When the S&D finished constructing its newly doubled line between Midford and Radstock in July 1894, the old Foxcote box, possibly renamed by then "Braysdon and Writhlington", had been demolished and a new one built slightly to the south-west on the other side of the road bridge. The new down line used the site of the Writhlington siding for much of the way between the colliery and Radstock, and a new east-facing curve was put in to serve the pit-head, joining a new siding laid beside the main line. The old westerly curve now terminated in a short headshunt and was eventually removed altogether in the 1950s. The new signalbox stood within the triangular arrangement of tracks formed by the old and new curves into the colliery.

The box, called simply "Writhlington", was of blue brick with a timber and glass superstructure rather like that at Wellow also built at the time of doubling. The earlier box would seem to have been one of the single-storey wooden huts used as signal cabins at such places as Midford, Wellow and Radstock before the line was doubled. Being merely a colliery box the new building was not decorated with the fine ornamental barge boards and finials found on similar boxes elsewhere on the line and, unusually, it had windows all the way round. From it the signalman controlled the two collieries' sidings as well as breaking up the main line section between Radstock and Wellow. There were nineteen levers (with five spare) operating the usual distant, home and starting signals on both lines. There were two trailing crossovers in the main line section providing a loop of about a hundred and fifty yards' length. It was from the sidings in 1936 that an errant tank engine ran away in the direction of Bath, following misplaced heroism by its crew, ultimately to dismember Midford signalbox and several unfortunate coal wagons!

Braysdown colliery closed in 1959 and the sidings were removed. In 1966, the year that the S&D closed, the steam winding engine at Writhlington was replaced by the electric one from Norton Hill, and the pit remained in production. The section of line into Radstock was kept in use as a siding for the coal trains, which for five more years continued to travel on that small piece of the S&D to the old Great Western line at the new Radstock junction, en route to Portishead power station. The signalbox was not sufficiently fortunate to last so long. And the short blustery day of March 6th was already turning into a grey dusk...

Opposite – A plan of Writhlington sidings c1890 showing the site of the original signalbox and the alterations required for the doubling of the main line.

Overleaf is a grand view of the pithead winding gear at Writhlington photographed in August 1970 by Philip Fowler.

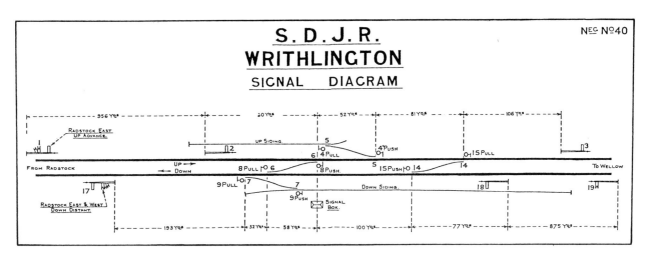

It was not until half past three that afternoon that Radstock offered two beats and three on the block bell. This code materialised as the two Ivatt tanks which had earlier worked the other Last Train along the branch. They were returning, coupled together, to Bath shed for the last time.

Night was gathering when, shortly before six, the southbound RCTS special was signalled into section from Wellow to repeat in the dusk the grinding crossover exercise with handsignalman, clamps and pilotman. And very soon afterwards the northbound SLS special returned, working hard against the gradient, the chain of carriage lights snaking around the contours. On the smokebox door of the leading locomotive swung a wreath, a cardboard sign inside the circlet of laurel still lettered in blue : 'Last Train to Bournemouth'.

And as the fading echoes of the wheelbeats were swallowed up into the night, in the resounding silence that lingered, signalman Horder recorded the passing in rule book prose, terminating the precise columns of bell codes and timings with a poetry that said more than any fancy epitaph. At a quarter to seven he received and noted the last ringing beats of the block bell from Radstock, 7-5-5 – "Closing Box". Then at seven o'clock he and signalman Dance signed off in the train register. With a final flourish of his biro copperplate script he wrote simply:

Writhlington Box taken out of use

Farewell S & D J R

Bowler hats in the foreground, cloth caps to the rear. Salter's Home Mills at Trowbridge, a majestic architectural testament to the industrial age, dating from 1862. The last working mill in the town, it closed in 1982.

Wiltshire Libraries

9

THE HALT IS WAITING YET

The end had been a long time coming. The Railway Age had faltered with the shattering impact on society of the First World War, and emerged from the Second truly unprepared for a changed world. The paradoxical landscapes of rural tranquility and industrial intrusion that we have found in eastern Somerset provoke echoes of the turmoil and disorder into which everyday life has been thrown by the despoliation of the land, by the growth and decay of industry and transport systems. When the first pit in Radstock wound its first coal to the surface in 1763, the countrymen and women came to accept it as part of the landscape, and adapted themselves to the living that was to be had from it. The communities became reconciled over the years to the upheaval of their agricultural traditions. This acceptance was by no means mute and meek however, being marked many times over by movements of discontent. For example, in the more industrialised country areas like the Radstock coalfield and the wool factories of Trowbridge there was a flurry of agitation in the last years of the 1830s in support of the Chartists. This call for further reform of Parliamentary representation struck a chord in areas where large labouring populations were growing up in confrontation with the traditional land-owning aristocracy and the new industrial masters. Essentially it showed how unsatisfactory was the relationship between those who laboured and those who governed the labourers, a dissatisfaction that was suppressed, and transcended by co-operative effort in good times, and which came to the surface in bad. And was it any different when, after two hundred years, the local mining communities faced the final eradication of their livelihood in the 1960s and 70s, to the counterpoint of politicians' empty assurances? Or any different for the railwaymen whose working environment was so rudely and so abruptly destroyed? Do we learn anything by regarding the landscape as a map of man's arrogance?

To the north of the valley of the Radstock brook, was another in which ran a tributary, the eastwardly-winding Cam. The Cam gave its name to the old colliery village of Camerton. Beside the Cam had lain the main waterway of the Somersetshire Coal Canal, into which the

The last load. Miners had been at work here for 95 years.　　　　　　　　　　Bath & West Evening Chronicle

Radstock arm for some years had connected. In the district around Camerton had been the most northerly of the Somerset coalfield's pits – Withy Mills, Lower Conygre, Bengrove... Here, by the early years of the nineteenth century, the countryside had been transformed by the arrival of the pit-head, the canal and the tramroad; and the local farming community had recast themselves as miners, boatmen, waggonwrights and boilersmiths.

At that time the Rev. John Skinner was Rector of Camerton Parish. As a disillusioned and plainly irascible old man, having sought for much of his life a reconciliation of the old ways and the new, having tried to make himself at one with the villagers, and finally having failed to find the peace he had prayed for, he ended his own life with a shotgun. A lengthy journal however, apparently his only confidante and comfort in life, he preserved for us.

His observations reveal a cultured mind bludgeoned by the insensitivity of his neighbours, and by a way of country life desperately accommodating itself to sudden and violent change through the destructive oblivions of ale and self-interest. And in much the same way as modern museum cultures seek lessons from the past to make the present more tolerable, John Skinner found his solace in the ancient and pre-history of Camerton. The Bath Turnpike Commissioners, debating the merits of Radstock Hill as a candidate for their attentions, frustrated and upset him. The Coal Canal claimed the lives of his parishioners who fell into it on their way home from the inn, or who threw themselves in for want of any other purpose. Lucky for him that he did not live to see the advent of the railway, for it was only ten months after he died that the Great Western opened its main line from Bristol to Bath. What he did see was bad enough.

'While writing in my study I saw numbers of men, at least fifty, cross the Park in front of my study window to go down to the pits at Camerton. I had learnt that the colliers meant to make a rise... I then walked to Clan Down, having heard that there had been a mob of the colliers assembled there yesterday, and that the Riot Act was read by Mr. James [the Timsbury magistrate]... I saw all was quiet on the Down, and the Steam Engine working, as I approached the pit. I walked thither, and found the Radstock Rioters, for I can call them by no other name, had gone on to Paulton...' (Dec 1830).

John Skinner's involvement with the Turnpike Trust may seem out of character amidst all this confusion, but it was Captain George Scobell who had persuaded him to attend the Commissioners' meetings. Captain Scobell was a man abreast of his time, a proprietor of local coal pits. He knew the railway had to come. He had given active support to the Radstock, Shaftesbury & Poole in 1825, to the Bath & Weymouth Great Western Union in 1836, and he became a director of the Wilts, Somerset & Weymouth in 1844. His thirty years' labour bore fruit with the Great Western's coal branch of 1854. Skinner, however, was something of an anachronism like his Roman pavement at Wellow, and his beloved Celtic burial chamber at Shoscombe. Life went on without him. The relentless railway passed him by.

And now the railway has gone from much of the land. Before and between the wars the companies tried to combat their decline by opening local halts, attending too late to the real needs of the 'happy cheese-growers', serving communities who had been petitioning for their own stations for years. Down the length of both the S&D and the Wilts, Somerset & Weymouth line, the spaces between the stations were filled in. A few small platforms of timber or concrete were put up to attract the traveller who was eagerly eyeing the alternative opportunities of the open road, the Austin 7 and the charabanc. The petrol fume was being discharged across the face of Camelot's quiet beauty.

A typical halt, built in 1937 of old creosoted sleepers, is Dilton Marsh on the Salisbury branch of the Wilts, Somerset & Weymouth near Westbury. The nearby village, spread out along the road, used to have the highest upstream cloth mill on the Biss. New estates surround the railway today, which climbs up from Westbury on a lengthy embankment. The halt was made with one platform on the north side of the road overbridge and one on the south side. It is one of the last survivors and earned immortality when it struck the late John Betjeman in autumnal mood:

Was it worth keeping the Halt open,
We thought as we looked at the sky
Red through the spread of the cedar-tree,
With the evening train gone by?

Yes, we said, for in summer the anglers use it,
Two and sometimes three
Will bring their catches of rods and poles and perches
To Westbury, home for tea.

There isn't a porter. The platform is made of sleepers.
The guard of the last up-train puts out the light
And high over lorries and cattle the Halt unwinking
Waits through the Wiltshire night.

O housewife safe in the comprehensive churning
Of the Warminster launderette!
O husband down at the depot with car in car-park!
The Halt is waiting yet.

Dilton Marsh Halt in the 1960s before the platforms were shortened, the lamps replaced by more advanced designs and the fixed distant signal taken away. Wiltshire Libraries

The S&D was buried a hundred and seven years after its birth, yet Dilton Marsh and the rest of the Wilts, Somerset & Weymouth have led a charmed life and survive, emasculated but still with the branch to Radstock, and a remnant of the East Somerset Railway which ran from Wells to Witham. There have been changes: the main line across Farmer Brown's fields was singled south of Castle Cary in 1968; Melksham station, closed in 1966, reopened nineteen years later. The Radstock branch now serves a wagon repair workshop descended from a firm established in the town by Ernest Marcroft in 1909. The line peters out in the town centre, hidden behind a grassy bank not far beyond its original terminus. Over the way, three very old men sit on a bench outside the new houses, built where the S&D used to run. They talk with lively gesticulations, tapping their sticks on the ground. Pipe smoke drifts from the group, the sudden aroma caught on a gentle current of air. Clean new road improvements with crisp kerbs surround and mark the sites of the town's infamous level crossings.

And on the East Somerset branch we find the final irony, for it is along this line, built by one of the most minor of the local Somerset railway companies, that the limestone, blasted from the face of eastern Mendip, is carried away. Unlike the building-stone workings of Bath and Portland which have contributed to some of the noblest architecture in the country, the quarries and rail connections at Merehead and Whatley have received major investment in recent years. And the reason is not hard to find. For this stone is crushed and used in the construction of man's most enduring technological vanity – the road.

> And when all the horrible roads are finally done for,
> And there's no more petrol left in the world to burn,
> Here to the Halt from Salisbury and from Bristol
> Steam trains will return.

Ex GWR 4-6-0 No 6943 "Farnley Hall", with 0-6-2 tank No 5689 banking at the rear, climbs past Dilton Marsh with a train from South Wales to Portsmouth. Photographed by R. E. Toop on May 12th 1956.

A Railway Chronology

RA – Royal Assent (confirmation of Parliamentary powers)
Op – Opened   Cl – Closed

1731   Ralph Allen's tramroad, Combe Down – Widcombe Wharf, Bath Op.
1763   First coal wound at Old Pit, Radstock.
1794   Somersetshire Coal Canal RA 17/4/94.
        Kennet & Avon Canal (proposed as the Western Canal) RA 17/4/94.
1796   Dorset & Somerset Canal RA 24/3/96.
1804   First steam winding engine, Middle Pit, Radstock.
1805   Somersetshire Coal Canal Op throughout. Steam
/6   pumping engine at Combe Hay.
        First steam mill engine at Trowbridge.
1810   Kennet & Avon Canal Op throughout.
1811   First steam mill engine at Frome.
1824   Bristol & London Rail Road proposed.
1826   Radstock, Shaftesbury & Poole Rly proposed.
        Western Rly proposed.
1835   Great Western Rly RA 31/8/35.
1836   Bath & Weymouth Great Western Union Rly proposed. Melksham, Devizes & Great Western Union Rly proposed. Railroad proposed, Glastonbury Canal Wharf – Bruton, branch Cole – Wincanton.
1841   Great Western Rly, Bath – Chippenham and thus throughout Op 30/6/41.
1844   Wilts & Somerset Rly proposed then altered to Wilts, Somerset & Weymouth Rly. Somersetshire Midland Rly proposed (Bruton – Wells – Glastonbury – Highbridge).
1845   Wilts, Somerset & Weymouth Rly RA 30/6/45. London, Newbury & Bath Direct Rly and London, Devizes & Bridgewater Direct Western Rly proposed by Kennet & Avon Canal.
        Bath, Wells & Exeter Rly proposed. Great West of England or South Western & Exeter Extension Rly proposed. Salisbury & Yeovil Rly proposed.
        Lord Dalhousie's Board of Trade Rly Dept Report on Schemes in Wilts, Dorset & Somerset.
1846   Wilts, Somerset & Weymouth Rly Supplementary RA 3/8/46 (Devizes junction altered from Melksham to Holt, Salisbury junction altered from Upton Scudamore to Westbury, Bradford – Bathampton line authorised, deviations at Thingley, Frome and Dorchester).
        GWR Twerton – Timsbury – Radstock branch proposed. Exeter Great Western Rly proposed (Yeovil – Exeter, Bridport – Axminster).

1847   Proposals rejected by 53-day Parliamentary Committee, Chairman William Deedes : WS&WR Compton – Wilton (Yeovil – Salisbury) and Bleadon – Blandford lines, Bristol & Exeter Rly Bleadon – Blandford, London & South Western Rly Bleadon – Blandford, GWR Yeovil – Bridport – Exeter. Berks & Hants Rly Reading – Hungerford Op 21/12/47.
1848   Proposals agreed by Committee previous year, given RA this year : LSWR Salisbury & Yeovil, LSWR Exeter Yeovil & Dorchester, B&ER Durston – Castle Cary, Berks & Hants Extension Rly (Hungerford – Devizes), WS&WR improved line Frome – Bruton.
        WS&WR Thingley – Westbury Op 5/9/48.
1850   WS&WR absorbed by GWR.
        Westbury – Frome Op 7/10/50.
1851   WS&WR absorption RA 3/7/51.
        Westbury – Warminster Op 9/9/51.
1852   Frome Yeovil & Weymouth Rly RA 30/6/52.
        Somerset Central Rly RA 17/6/52.
        Kennet & Avon Canal taken over by GWR 30/6/52.
        South Midland Rly proposed (Mangotsfield – Radstock – Bournemouth).
1853   Mandamus at Somerset Assizes Queens Bench for completion of Bradford – Bathampton line.
1854   GWR extension of time to complete WS&W line RA 31/7/54.
        LSWR Salisbury – Yeovil RA 7/8/54 (powers already obtained had lapsed).
        Somerset Central Rly Glastonbury – Highbridge Op 17/8/54.
        GWR Frome-Radstock Op 14/11/54.
        South Wales & Southampton Rly proposed (Weston – Cheddar – Wincanton).
1855   SCR Burnham, Wells extensions RA 30/7/55.
        Dorset Central Rly proposed (Wimborne – Wyke Champflower, on WS&W line).
1856   GWR Warminster – Salisbury Op 31/6/56, Frome – Yeovil Op 1/9/56.
        LSWR Yeovil – Exeter RA 21/7/56, SCR Glastonbury – Cole, on WS&W line RA 21/7/56, DCR Wimborne – Blandford RA 29/7/56.
        East Somerset Rly Witham, on WS&W line – Shepton Mallet RA 5/6/56.
1857   GWR Yeovil – Weymouth Op 20/1/57, Trowbridge – Bathampton Op 2/2/57, Devizes – Holt Op 1/7/57.
        ESR Shepton Mallet – Wells RA 27/7/57, DCR Blandford – Bruton RA 10/8/57.
1858   ESR Witham – Shepton Mallet Op 9/11/58.

1859   SCR Glastonbury – Wells Op 3/3/59.
1860   LSWR Salisbury – Exeter Op throughout 19/7/60.
       DCR Op 1/11/60.
1862   ESR Shepton – Wells Op 1/3/62. Berks & Hants Ext
       Rly Hungerford – Devizes Op 11/11/62.
       SCR and DCR amalgamated RA 7/8/62, new title
       Somerset & Dorset Rly 1/9/62.
1863   Bristol & North Somerset Rly RA 21/7/63.
       Somerset Coal Rly proposed (Wincanton – Timsbury).
1865   Bath & Radstock Rly proposed. B&NSR proposal
       Farrington Gurney (B&NS) – Evercreech (S&D).
1870   GWR agreement with B&NSR and coal proprietors to
       lay narrow gauge between Radstock and Salisbury.
1871   S&DR Extension to Bath RA 21/8/71.
1873   B&NSR Bristol – Radstock Op 3/9/73.
1874   GWR Wilts, Somerset & Weymouth line, gauge
       narrowed, Thingley – Weymouth, Salisbury and
       Radstock branches. Also Westbury – Frome doubled.
       Holt Junction station Op 1/4/74.
       ESR amalgamated with GWR and gauge narrowed.
       S&DR Evercreech – Bath Op 20/7/74.
1876   B&ER amalgamated with GWR.
       S&DR leased jointly to Midland and LSWR (new title
       Somerset & Dorset Joint Railway) RA 13/7/76.
1880   GWR Witham – Castle Cary doubled.
1881   GWR Castle Cary – Yeovil doubled.
1882   Berks & Hants Ext Rly amalgamated with GWR.
1883   GWR renewed proposals to build Stert – Westbury and
       Castle Cary – Langport lines.
1884   B&NSR amalgamated with GWR.
1894   S&DJR most of main line now doubled.
1900   GWR Stert – Westbury fully Op 1/10/00. B&H Ext
       doubled.
1902   North Somerset Light Railway proposed (Clutton –
       Camerton – Limpley Stoke).
1904   Somersetshire Coal Canal abandoned, GWR Camerton
       – Limpley Stoke branch RA 15/8/04.

1905   Last Bradford-on-Avon cloth mill closed.
       Lacock Halt and Staverton Halt Op 16/10/05.
       GWR Castle Cary – Charlton Mackrell Op single line
       1/7/05.
1906   GWR Direct route London – Westbury – Taunton fully
       Op 2/7/06.
       Avoncliff Halt Op 9/7/06, Beanacre Halt and
       Broughton Gifford Halt Op 30/10/06.
1922   Grouping of railway companies.
1932   Strap Lane Halt Op 18/7/32.
1933   Westbury and Frome by-passes Op 1/1/33.
1937   Dilton Marsh Halt Op 1/6/37.
1941   Strap Lane Halt Cl 6/10/41 (reopened 16/12/46 finally
       Cl 5/6/50).
1948   Nationalisation of railway companies.
1955   Beanacre Halt and Broughton Gifford Halt Cl 7/2/55,
       Salisbury branch stations except Warminster and
       Dilton Marsh Cl 19/9/55.
1959   Bristol – Frome Cl to passengers 2/11/59.
1962   Charlton Mackrell, Keinton Mandeville and other
       stations on that line Cl 10/9/62.
1965   Last Frome cloth mill closed.
1966   Somerset & Dorset line Cl 6/3/66.
       Lacock Halt, Melksham, Holt Jnc, Staverton Halt,
       Devizes branch Cl 18/4/66, line singled between
       Thingley and Bradford Jnc.
       Bathampton, Limpley Stoke, Witham, Sparkford,
       Marston Magna Cl 3/10/66.
1968   Castle Cary – Dorchester singled throughout by
       9/6/68.
       Radstock – Bristol fully Cl 10/7/68.
1970   Merehead stone quarry redeveloped.
1973   Last Radstock colliery closed, Writhlington.
1982   Last Trowbridge cloth mill closed.
1984   Original WS&WR station building at Trowbridge
       demolished due to 'major structural faults'.
1985   Melksham station reopened to passengers 13/5/85.

Acknowledgments

Much of the basic historical material in this book has been gathered over the years from the published sources listed in the bibliography. My own exploration of the areas in question and further delving into original documents have stimulated a continuing fascination with the subject.

A few particular sources of information should be mentioned here – the Bath & Weymouth Railway saga (Chapter 1) was extracted from contemporary reports and advertisements in the Bath Chronicle, as were the opening of the Wilts, Somerset & Weymouth Railway to Westbury (Chapter 4), the advertisement for Radstock coal and the celebration of Thomas Pilditch's wedding (Chapter 5), the glimpse of Queen Victoria at Trowbridge and the opening of the Bruton Railway (Chapter 6).

The story of William Brown's fields was reconstructed from parish and census records and from original documents in my own collection. I have quoted freely from Lord Dalhousie's 1845 Board of Trade Report and the transcript of Mr. Cockburn's speech in support of the L&SWR interest at the 1847 Parliamentary Committee hearing (Chapters 3, 4 and 5). The Edward Thomas quotations come from his _Collected Poems_ and _In Pursuit of Spring_. The other authors quoted are included in the bibliography.

Photographs not otherwise credited are from my own collection. The drawings on the title pages of Parts 1, 2 and 3 are based on photographs of Trowbridge. These are, respectively, a view across the fields from the west showing the goods shed, late C19th (Wiltshire Libraries); the original signalbox c1900 (Charles Jones collection); the demolition of the station building in 1984 (Wiltshire Times).

Many people have helped to produce this book and I am very grateful to them all – firstly to the publishers, Alan and Tim, for their consideration and encouragement; to everyone who read and suggested amendments to the manuscript; to C. L. Caddy, Richard Casserley, Philip Fowler, John Froud, Chris Handley, Charles Jones, Colin Maggs, Dennis Rendell, John Smith, R. E. Toop, and M. J. Tozer for the use of material from their collections; to Robin Atthill, Sean Bolan, Dr Peter Cattermole, Trefor David, Jonathan Edwards, Chris Osment and Ivo Peters for responding to my queries; to Rev. R. Simmons for helping me to find William Brown; and to British Rail for permission to photograph the bridge near North Barrow; to Mike Arlett and Brendan Mulryan for their encouragement, and Dave and Vicky for their typewriter; to the staff of the Somerset Record Office, Bath Reference Library, Wiltshire Local Studies Library at Trowbridge, Mr K.W. Merrett of Melksham & District Historical Association and Mr J. Bryan of Swindon Railway Museum for their assistance; to the following for permission to quote from copyright texts – Faber & Faber Ltd, publishers of W. H. Auden's _The English Auden : Poems, Essays and Dramatic Writings 1927-1939_; John Murray (Publishers) Ltd publishers of John Betjeman's 'Dilton Marsh Halt' and 'Distant View of a Provincial Town' in his _Collected Poems_; Hodder & Stoughton Ltd, publishers of Monica Hutchings' _The Chronicles of Church Farm_; British Rail, copyright holders of Maxwell Fraser's _Somerset_; to the Editor, David Flintham, for permission to reproduce and quote extracts from the _Bath Chronicle_; to the Somerset Record Office (S.R.O.) for permission to use material from the _Western Flying Post_ and the deposited plans of the Bath & Weymouth and Wilts, Somerset & Weymouth Railways; to the National Railway Museum and the Borough of Thamesdown for permission to reproduce photographs of the Wilts, Somerset & Weymouth Railway seal and opening-day handbill held at Swindon Railway Museum; to the Director of the Wiltshire County Council Library and Museum Service for permission to reproduce photographs in their care; and finally to Paddy, Katie and Benna for their special help.

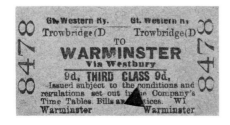

Bibliography

The Curious Past – Robin Atthill, Wessex Press
Old Mendip – Robin Atthill, David and Charles
Some of Our Old Pictures – Chris Howell
Round Here in Them Days – Chris Howell
I Have Heard Tell – Chris Howell
Journal of a Somerset Rector – Rev. John Skinner, OUP
The History of the Parish of Radstock – G. A. V. Foster
Castle Cary – Michael McGarvie, Avalon Industries
The Book of Frome – Michael McGarvie, Barracuda
The Book of Trowbridge – Kenneth Rogers, Barracuda
Rural Life in Wessex 1500-1900 – J. H. Bettey, Moonraker
A Tourist's Guide to Somersetshire – R. N. Worth, Edward Stanford (1894)
The Coal-field of North Somersetshire – Seward W. Brice, Bemrose & Lothian (1867)
The History of the Somerset Coalfield – C. G. Down & A. J. Warrington, David and Charles
My Life as a Somerset Miner – A. J. Parfitt, Durham West & Sons
The Woollen Industry of South West England – K. G. Ponting, Adams & Dart
Wiltshire and Somerset Woollen Mills – Kenneth Rogers, Pasold Research Fund
Warp and Weft – The Story of the Somerset & Wilts Woollen Industry – Kenneth Rogers, Barracuda Books
The Somersetshire Coal Canal & Railways – Kenneth R. Clew, David and Charles
The Dorset & Somerset Canal – Kenneth R. Clew, David and Charles
The Kennet & Avon Canal – Kenneth R. Clew, David and Charles
Railway Bridges, Culverts & Stations – J. W. Grover, E. & F. N. Spon (1870)
The Somerset & Dorset Railway, a Tourist's Descriptive Guide – D. H. Gale, Keene (1874)
The History of a Railway (Salisbury & Yeovil) – Louis H. Ruegg, Sherborne Journal (1878)
A Regional History of the Railways of Great Britain Vol 1 The West Country – David St John Thomas, David and Charles
History of the Great Western Railway – E. T. MacDermot (revised C. R. Clinker) Ian Allan
A Pictorial Record of Great Western Architecture – A. Vaughan, OPC
The Camerton Branch – Colin Maggs & Gerry Beale, Wild Swan
The Bath to Weymouth Line – Colin Maggs, Oakwood Press
The East Somerset Railway 1858-1972 – Colin Maggs, Avon-Anglia
The Bristol & North Somerset Railway 1863-1884 – David Warnock, Avon-Anglia
The Bristol & North Somerset Railway since 1884 – D. W. Warnock & R. G. Parsons, Avon-Anglia
Railways in Wells – R. Hayes & M. Shaw, HST
Holt Junction – Holt Magazine Supplement
A Last Look at Holt Junction – Holt Magazine Supplement
The Newbury Railway – C. G. Down & A. J. Warrington, IRS
Track Layout Diagrams of the GWR and BR – R. A. Cooke
The Somerset & Dorset Railway – Robin Atthill, David and Charles
The Picture History of the Somerset & Dorset Railway – Robin Atthill, David and Charles
The Somerset & Dorset Railway – D. S. Barrie & C. R. Clinker, Oakwood Press
The Somerset & Dorset – An English Cross-Country Railway – Ivo Peters, OPC
An Historical Survey of the Somerset & Dorset Railway – C. W. Judge & C. R. Potts, OPC
The Railways and Tramways of Radstock – Chris Handley, S&DRMT
All About Midsomer Norton S&DJR – John Childs, HMRS
The Somerset & Dorset at Midford – Mike Arlett, Millstream Books
The Somerset & Dorset Then and Now – Mac Hawkins, Patrick Stephens

Avon Valley - Autumn 1986